CW00458594

CLOUDS OF HAPPINESS

The highs and lows of domestic life

HELEN BROWN

ANGUS
& ROBERTSON
PUBLISHERS

By the same author
Don't Let Me Put You Off
Confessions of a Bride Doll
Tomorrow, When It's Summer

Helen Brown has been writing for a living since she was sixteen. She started as a cadet reporter on **The Dominion**, worked on an English magazine and then returned to New Zealand to freelance. Now a much-syndicated newspaper columnist, she is currently a feature writer for the **Sunday Star**. She also appears regularly on "Beauty and the Beast".

She has two children, Robin and Lydia. Her oldest son, Sam, was killed in a traffic accident in 1983.

CONTENTS

ANGUS & ROBERTSON PUBLISHERS

Unit 4, Eden Park, 31 Waterloo Road,
North Ryde, NSW, Australia 2113, and
16 Golden Square, London W1R 4BN,
United Kingdom

First published in Australia
by Angus & Robertson Publishers in 1988

Copyright © Helen Brown 1988

National Library of Australia
Cataloguing-in-publication data.

Brown, Helen, 1954-
    Clouds of happiness.

    ISBN 0 207 15939 4.

    1. Family — Anecdotes, facetiae, satire,
    etc. I. Title.

306.8'7'0207

Typeset in 10pt Palatino by Keyset
Printed in Australia by The Book Printer

1

The man who liked my pink curved legs

I SHOULD have known the removal men would arrive the day the baby got two new teeth and an ear infection. The same day our nine year old decided there was no way he'd leave town.

I was still wearing my dressing gown when their giant hairy knuckles rapped on the door. Past caring, I slung the baby on my hip to let them into the house.

The baby is already developing a depressing fascination with macho men. When she clapped eyes on their shapely bronzed legs, she batted her lids and glowed like a neon sign. It was nothing to do with her temperature.

'Dadda!' she crowed, throwing out her chubby arms in welcome.

The two removal men reddened and studied their hobnails. I tried to explain how she calls all men that name. (It doesn't do wonders for my reputation, but I do get invitations to parties.) They trudged through the place.

'Is it all going?' said the tall one with eyes like pools of oil.

'Everything except that big floral sofa, the little desk in there that's falling apart, the big desk with model paint all over it, the wardrobe with radio station stickers on it and the rubber plant.'

They swung into action, wrapping everything we owned in yellow paper and stuffing it into boxes. It made me realise how much genuine junk we had — a squashed sun hat, three tea-stained cushions circa 1973 and several rusty cake tins, for a start.

I whisked away a tiny glass dish full of solidified salt and our decaying range of spices before they could see them (I hoped).

'Never mind,' said the thin blond one. 'I've seen worse.'

To express my gratitude, I put on my son's Dire Straits record. The removal men turned it off in favour of the rock station on the kitchen radio. They seemed to feel some empathy with 'When The Going Gets Tough, The Tough Get Going'. I was amazed by their silent efficiency. Every box was labelled according to its contents — 'Books, etc', 'Misc', 'Misc'. Several bore another word I couldn't decipher.

I tried to help by hurling jackets, shoes and handbags at them. But I soon discovered the only way to make removal men whistle is to make them coffee and muffins. They hadn't heard of Germaine Greer.

As the day wore on, the place began to look less like our home and more like a house that had belonged to people who couldn't hang wallpaper straight.

I could hear a removal man playing space invaders in our son's bedroom. He was very good. It was the perfect time for me to get rid of the ugly little table in the hall. It was pink with curved legs like a spider's. I'd tried to scrape the paint off it once, but it hadn't worked. I'd had to cover it with a lace tablecloth.

My husband had expressed affection for it, but I was certain he wouldn't miss the thing.

I carried it down to the basement, hurled it into the shadows and hit a removal man where it hurts most.

'I'm terribly sorry!' I said. 'I had no idea you were in there.'

He looked at his injury, at me and, finally, at the weapon.

'It's quite a nice little table,' he said.

'Would you like it?' I asked.

He picked it up, examined it and smiled.

'I'm starting up house shortly,' he mumbled bashfully.

Inspired with enthusiam, I offered him the sofa, the two desks, the rubber plant and the nest of panel heaters we'd found under the bed. But he was content with the table. I had the feeling it was going to a good home.

There are many complications about moving to another city. Not the least of them is selling your house. We had spent years looking for that place. When we finally walked up the path under the dreamy fronds to our gingerbread cottage, I was prepared to break the bank for it. And did.

We had been looking for a bargain. They don't make our kind of house for our kind of money. We always end up in something with Drawbacks. This one had access down an almost vertical zigzag. We didn't care.

When we decided to leave that house, we were certain someone would fall in love with it in just the same way. They didn't. Prospective buyers grizzled about the spouting, the decor (*my* decor!), the access, the lack of garaging, the plumbing, the weatherboards and even the stove. It got so bad, I had to restrain myself from flinging my arms around the ankles of every person who shuffled disdainfully through the shagpile.

'If only you'd put it on the market a month ago,' one agent said. 'People were on transfer then. Houses were going like hot cakes. Which company is it your husband works for?'

For the umpteenth time, I explained it was my job, not his, that was taking us out of town. The agents said it was a buyer's market. With interest rates the way they were, the glut of houses and the economic situation, I had to believe them.

'Yours is just the sort of house that's slow to move right now,' another said. 'The cheapest ones are no problem and mansions are in demand.'

I sighed and looked at her leather mini-skirt and plunging silk blouse. A woman her age should know better. I knew there was no point in telling her the bus stop was very close and the neighbours were lovely — one had even helped to deliver our baby. She'd simply say there wasn't much demand for neighbours who deliver babies. I wished she would go away.

Someone did come along eventually. I never met them, but the agent said they didn't like the decor and the access and the stove. So they made a silly offer. We had to take it.

Soon after, we were in a new city looking for another house. We saw one with four bedrooms, verandahs, a wall oven and a machine down the kitchen plug hole that devours anything. We loved it. But it was out of our range.

Once again, we began to sense we were on the lookout for a bargain. We could afford a palace on a dismal slope 150 kilometres out of town, or a shed on a street where the school was good. The agents understood our depression.

'But you must realise,' one of them said, 'with money so freely available and the price of land going up, it is a seller's market.'

I had to believe him. Once again, we'd have to compromise. We went to see a gracious two-storeyed property. Perfect condition and the owners were desperate to sell. Only trouble was it was built on a motorway. The whole place shuddered every time a car went past.

'Does the traffic noise worry you?' I yelled at the owner, who was pretending to dig the garden.

'What?'

'I said DOES THE NOISE GET TO YOU?'

'Oh, only first thing in the morning and around six at night.'

I looked at my watch. It was 3 p.m.

We found another nice place we could almost afford. But it had two bedrooms. It wasn't long before we learned to translate landagentese. Elegant: overpriced. Sunny: exposed to the neighbours. Charming: run down. Secluded: overgrown. Potential: destroyed. Elevated: on a mountaintop. Spacious: someone has put a third bedroom in the basement. Private: damp. Wide view: exposed to the road. Handy to all amenities: on the main road to the airport. Convenient: next door to a massage parlour. Cosy: previous owner (an accountant) has sold off the front garden and built a multi-storey apartment block there.

I was beginning to think we had seen it all. Until an agent gave us the address of something in a very classy neighbourhood. We weren't expecting much for that price in that area. But when we got there, we couldn't believe our eyes. The house stood in two pieces on the lawn. Someone had sawn it in half — right up the back passage.

Eventually, we found a modest villa with no apparent problems. But whenever we move into a new house, we discover a dastardly secret. The land agent manages to sell it to us long before we realise there's no water pressure, the weatherboards are made of cardboard and the piles are hellbent on reaching Spain.

This time, it was the garage. There's nothing wrong with the garage itself. It's more of a carport, really. At some stage, someone dug out the area under the house to put a car there. A nice, sensible, civilised thing to do.

It was a tantalising feature to a family who had survived without a garage for several years. Although the car had a rust problem that was now terminal, we were pleased it could eke out the rest of its days in comparative luxury.

As soon as we signed up for the house, we nudged the car's creaking chassis into the garage. We slept easily that night, knowing at last the car was getting the care it deserved. I made a silent promise that I'd dig the old hamburgers out from the cracks in the seats some day. Next morning, I woke to a terrible bellow.

'Mum! The garage is full of water!'

I sprang out of bed, wrapped a dressing gown around the appropriate parts and dashed outside. Sure enough, the entire floor was covered with brown liquid. There must have been a storm last night, I thought. I'd been so tired I hadn't heard a thing.

'Nothing to worry about,' I said. 'I'll sweep it out later.'

Towards the end of the day, I took the garden broom down to the garage. The water level had gone up an inch or two. So I called a plumber who materialised, miraculously, half an hour later and pumped it out.

Next morning, it was a rush to get to school and work. I shoved cereal and fruit juice into the mouths lined up at the breakfast bar and hurried outside.

'Hey, Mum!' The tone had that combination of excitement and horror I dread. 'Look!'

Small waves were lapping around the hub caps. In a matter of hours, the whole car would be submerged.

'Hope it's amphibious,' a kindly passerby remarked.

'But we can't even get in!' I almost sobbed at the kid. 'We'll need waders or snorkel gear.'

There are times when the combination of nine-year-old genius and a rusty station wagon works wonders. I watched in awe as he simply opened the hatchdoor and scrambled over the back seat into the front.

'C'mon!' he called.

I drew a breath and followed — briefcase, handbag, coat, seven-denier pantyhose and all. I prayed the tide hadn't reached the engine yet. We were in luck.

The day takes on a grim prospect when you know your basement is full of water that has no reason to stop rising. Would we be dining on the roof of the house that night?

I rang the plumber and got an answerphone. I tried two others who were out. I finally found one who said he'd look at the job, but didn't. The car seemed to accept its place back on the street.

As days went by, the flood turned into a murky swimming pool — and a fascinating new toy for the baby. She spent happy hours standing on the verandah throwing priceless household items into the deep.

'That's my *Roget's Thesaurus!*' I cried.

'Never mind,' said a visiting friend. 'It was an old edition.'

After several more hysterical calls to plumbers, I began to stop panicking. So what if the dam burst and we were flushed down the street on top of the neighbours? Or if it attracted mosquitoes and we got dysentery? Or if hippopotamuses escaped from the zoo and decided to breed down there? I eventually got hold of the first plumber again.

'Would you repeat your name, please?' he said.

'Helen — as in Troy. As in the face that launched a thousand station wagons.'

He rang two days later to explain why it would cost one thousand dollars to fix. Something to do with soggy soil and the lack of drains and council permissions.

'On the other hand, you could buy a pump,' he said. 'That's what the previous owners had down there. It's all wired up for one.'

As I cast my mind back to the first time we saw the house, I recalled a black rubber hose coming out of the garage. I had assumed it was something to do with handymen. If only he had told us, we'd have thought no less of him or his house.

After we'd bought a new pump, the car returned to its rightful place. With any luck, the floods will stick with Noah where they belong. And I'll get around to digging out the old hamburgers.

2

How the baby went to Istanbul, almost

THERE ARE certain things you need to find when you move to a new city — the nearest supermarket, the fastest way to work, the safest way home from school. It was so time-consuming, I began to wish we'd stayed in the old town where I'd known what time the milk arrived and that Tuesday was rubbish night.

On top of everything else, I had to find a doctor. The baby's symptoms were unmistakable — red face, streaming nose and a tendency to pull her right ear. An ear infection that antibiotics would quickly clear.

A friend had given me names of suitable GPs — the sort who wouldn't commit major surgery the moment you lay on their couch. But when it came to the crunch, I headed for the medical centre around the corner. I was relieved to find it was a converted house with brick paving outside. It looked quite friendly.

Kids always perk up and act superhealthy when they go to the doctor. The baby was no exception. She tore up a magazine, made animated goos at a toddler and stuffed most of a red toy telephone down her throat.

Sometimes I think doctors like to make you wait. It's their way of reminding you how important they are. Lawyers and accountants have their own ways of being infuriating, but at least they work on the principle that your time is no less valuable than theirs.

When the nurse showed me into a little surgery, I assumed there would be more time to kill. I decided to change the baby's pants.

'A thrush infection, I see,' a voice boomed behind me.

I turned, startled to see a small, bearded man in shorts.

'I thought it was a nappy rash,' I said.

'You'll need a prescription for that,' he said, reaching for his pen.

So I'd landed myself a prescription-happy doctor. My defences were up.

7

'That *is* what you came here for?' he said, filling in a long silence.

'No, it's her ear.'

He peered suspiciously into both of them. Yes, they were red. He said carefully 'Some people don't approve of antibiotics . . .'

I was flattered to think he saw me as so advanced. I was about to tell him that although I understood the drawbacks of antibiotics and I certainly didn't think they should be handed out like lollies, I wouldn't be offended by a bottle of Amoxil right now.

'. . . and I'm one of them,' he added firmly.

I tried not to react, but I couldn't help feeling irritated, not to mention disappointed. I've read how people can respond when they're refused medicine they think they need. Rage, resentment, tears. I was determined not to behave like that.

'If I give her antibiotics, she'll be better in a couple of days,' he said. 'On the other hand, if we leave it to nature, she might also be better in a couple of days.'

I nodded. It was a confusing reversal of the usual stuff about ears being serious and needing immediate attention. He suggested painkiller in the meantime — and wrote out a prescription for antibiotics to be used if she got worse in the next day or so.

'Have you heard of Septrin?'

'No'.

'Good. It's an antibiotic.'

He was the sort of doctor I'd expect to meet barefooted in the Himalayas. Still, I had to admit the approach was refreshing. I'd never met a man so anti-antibiotics. I collected the painkiller from the chemist and stuck the antibiotic and thrush ointment prescriptions on a nail on the kitchen wall.

Feeling enthused, I bathed the baby's bottom in nature's disinfectant — a salt solution. It was almost healed next morning. Nature wasn't doing such a great job with her ear, however. It seemed unfair to let her suffer any more. I poured her first dose of Septrin with a tinge of regret. But maybe the twentieth century has something to offer, after all.

There are massive complications in being the parent of a toddler in this modern age. Have kids. Will travel. That's how it's supposed to be. If parents want to climb the Andes or hitchhike through Turkey, all you do is fling the baby on a backpack and the toddler under one arm and you're off.

Children aren't allowed to be a hindrance any more. They're there to enrich your already dazzling life. They will lie meekly in sardine-tin cots during your 36-hour flights to Paris, coo comfortably on the backs of camels as you traverse the Sahara and devour street-cooked curries in Delhi without so much as a burp.

Children are, after all, people who will gain much if you expose them to a lot of different experiences. But some people you can't take anywhere. The toddler really ought to be civilised. But we are enduring a slight problem phase. Toddlers should be chained to stumps for two years. Instead, people insist they're ready for public exposure. I begged to get a babysitter when Libby rang with a last-minute dinner invitation.

'But everyone is bringing their babies. There's Emma who's three weeks and Toby who's six months. There are a couple of older ones, too. And Simon is fourteen now. He'll look after them all.'

The lure of company and a night away from television was too great. I became a third-world mother and took my toddler to a dinner party.

'Isn't she sweet?' they said as she thundered through the house inciting rebellion among previously quiet, obedient children. 'Tall for her age, too.'

After she'd supervised mass jumping on mattresses, skiddings on the kitchen floor and a chippie snow storm, they were all put in bed. Miraculously, she was asleep in a matter of minutes.

Wondering why on earth I'd forked out so much in babysitting fees over the years, I sat down to a truly elegant meal. The chat was witty and interesting, ranging from politics in Fiji to second marriages. It's heartening to know that yesterday's broken home is today's extended family.

But Toby woke up after the oyster soup. His dad, being the useful modern sort, took him down the hall to bellow. It wasn't long before my offspring woke to join the chorus. Toby went back to sleep. Mine would not. She refused to have anything more to do with her travel cot, television, any of the helpful adults, or even Simon.

'Honestly, we don't mind her staying up if you don't,' they said as she perched on my knees while I ate pork and apricot casserole with one hand.

'GO HOME NOW!' said the person on my lap.

Not for the first time, I felt like a ventriloquist with a fiercely independent dummy. When the talk got back to Fiji, she squirmed wildly.

'We've all been through it,' they said as I ferretted through the fridge for something for her to eat.

'GO HOME!' she said, when she'd sunk a glass of milk and half a packet of biscuits.

Back at the table, she attempted to swing on my hoop earrings. I tried to smile graciously.

'Would you like to put her down for a cry? It won't worry us.'

I shrugged apologetically. They obviously hadn't heard my daughter's yell.

'HOME!'

'Not now, dear. Put my spoon back on the table. That's a good girl.'

'Would you like to see Mummy from another side?' said the man on my right. 'I'm used to children sitting on my knee.'

'NO!'

'You should get one of those little seats you can clip onto the table,' one of the women said. 'That way they're on your level.'

The two other men heartily offered less tasteful suggestions.

'Try putting her hand down the toaster. Then you tell the welfare it was an accident.'

Only some of the women could raise a polite smile. After a while, I started to feel comfortable again. Maybe it really was possible to enjoy conversation with a child on your knee at a table. I was three parts through telling a funny story, when she flipped my plate — pork, apricots and all — over the virgin white tablecloth. The stain was like a giant exploding star.

'It's all right,' the hostess said, scraping the residue back on my plate. 'It's not my best tablecloth. It will soak out. Probably.'

'HOME!'

The chocolate cake looked sumptuous. But it would have been like fighting Rambo without a machine gun.

'Are you sure you won't stay?' they said as I bundled her into the car. 'I suppose you know best.'

'HURRY UP!' growled the voice from the car seat.

At 11 p.m., she was still awake as I waited for the lights to turn green. I guess if I get the chance to go to Tibet, I'll do it alone.

How the baby went to Istanbul, almost

It's strange how quickly people forget. Those who had kids a while back forget the rigours of having a baby in the house. And those who choose never to have children at all might as well drive off in their BMWs and find another country to live in.

It's 5.30 p.m. There's a landslide of dishes on the kitchen bench. The baby has poured yoghurt over her head and is massaging it into her scalp. The nine year old is dressed up in his Cub gear and yelling for his woggle.

In another part of the house, I know the bath is nearly overflowing. Someone has emptied the entire contents of a soap powder packet over the floor and the loo is mysteriously choked with paper.

It's times like this that a calm, unworldly creature who has been perched on a stool sipping G and Ts for the past half-hour will clear her throat and say, 'Don't you ever sing to the baby?'

People who don't have kids are like those who belong to obscure religious sects. They seem to walk around in their own private bubbles of Nirvana. They're extremely well-meaning, but their eyes have an unrealistic glow from years of sleeping, talking and going out whenever they like.

People who don't have kids watch with indulgent smiles as you flap from one disaster to the next yelling cruel outrageous things at your offspring. 'You shouldn't tell him he'll end up sniffing glue if he goes down that alley,' they say coldly.

They know that if only you were a little more organised, more intelligent in your approach, the whole family would run more smoothly than the latest compact disc player, which they happen to have bought.

If and when they decide to have kids, which won't be till they own a house outright and have circumnavigated the world three times, they will show you how it's done.

They will read Dr Seuss to the baby while it's still in the womb, grow their own organic vegetables and take everyone on eight-day, uncomplaining treks through our national parks.

We hare off down the road ten minutes late for Cubs. My childless friend, who seems immune to the nerve-racking screams from the back seat, turns to me and says, 'Have you ever thought of educating them at home?'

There's no point in telling her that someone who has trouble adding up the milk money hardly feels equipped. People like her

11

are appalled that your kids have plugged their umbilical cords into the TV set.

'We don't let him watch anything violent,' I say.

'Yeah,' the child adds. 'Like the time that man's head came off and the blood spurted out and this other guy got this knife and . . . she made me turn it off. I'd seen the good bit, anyway.'

They think your kids are incredibly rude, bad mannered and poorly disciplined. They are probably right.

People who haven't reproduced stay up till midnight to discuss The Meaning Of Life. They think you're unbelievably dull when you crawl into bed at 9.30. They have oodles of energy left for passionate affairs, vegetarian diets and finding themselves.

Sometimes, in compassionate moments, they even have enough enthusiasm left to tell you how to sort out your pathetic existence. They'll say that What You Really Need To Do is:

(a) Get drunk. 'I mean completely blotto. Haven't you ever really let go?'
(b) Get your body in shape. 'Half an hour at the gym each day would do wonders.' (Which half hour?)
(c) Spend three weeks in New York. 'You really could do with some mental stimulation and I know some terrific people there.'

A few days later, somebody at our place decided to have a barbecue. At least, that's what I assumed was going on when the house was full of black smoke. I thought I'd ring Jonathan, who was probably feeling lonely the way single people do. He said he'd love to.

'When are you eating?' he asked.

'In about half an hour,' I said, allowing him oodles of time to get ready.

'But I couldn't possibly — not that early. I have to go for my run, and it would mess up my digestion something awful!'

In many ways, childless people are special and delightful. They think you have Jaffas stuck down your sofa because you're a free thinker. They believe you are poisoning your kids when you feed them instant pudding. They think you like to have food on your trousers.

They don't realise the last uninterrupted conversation you had with your husband was in 1973 when you said 'I think you'd better take me to the hospital now.' That the last decent sleep you had was some time in 1972. Yet they remain curious about your lifestyle, as if they suspect their state may be unrounded and somehow unfulfilled.

'Why don't you bring the baby to work?' said one associate when I told him of my childcare problems. 'She could sit over here under the window.'

It was on the tip of my tongue to tell him she'd sit for no more than thirty seconds. That in five minutes she'd have the room looking like Hiroshima on a bad day. But then, he'd only recently told me his wife was pregnant for the first time. He would soon find out.

3

Who are those people at the other table?

I GUESS it's understandable. Some of the yuppies are having such a great time, they want to pretend kids don't exist. Maybe it's fair enough, but I wish they'd let us know where the no-go areas are so we don't make mistakes.

The restaurant no longer caters for children. So why am I standing here with a baby on one hip and a nine year old at my side? The nine year old has combed his hair. I'd forgotten it was that colour under all the tangles. He's wearing a new shirt and new shoes on the right feet to bring us to this, the restaurant of his choice.

A woman in a purple lamé dress curls cobra-like behind the till and glares at the fruit of my loins.

'But I thought you were a family restaurant?' I say.

'Not any more.'

They can't have heard of us already. We're new in town. I'm tired and hungry. I don't want to spend the next hour driving around the streets looking for a place that takes kids.

'Could I see the menu?'

Her long red nails slide over the till to a stack of menus, hand-printed in self-conscious black ink. She fixes me with an amber eye and flashes one at me, daring me to faint at the prices. Duck for $19.95. Appetisers for ten dollars. I'm past caring.

'Do you have a high chair?'

'No,' she says firmly.

I'm beginning to hate the woman in purple lamé with her imitation gold chain, drag queen makeup and uppity ways. On the top left-hand corner of the menu, I see the stamp of the family restaurant chain that serves ordinary food at ordinary prices. The same symbol that we'd seen out on the turn-off. I'm getting so furious my manner has become ice queen calm.

Who are those people at the other table?

'Is there nothing for kids to eat?' I say.

'Nothing at all — unless you count fish and chips.'

'Why didn't you say?' I say, ignoring the possibility it could cost fifteen dollars a serve. 'We'll take it twice.'

She eyes me coolly, like a chess champion, and says, 'Have you booked a table?'

'No.' I sound like a member of the Royal Family. 'Do you think you could fit us in somewhere?'

'Not till seven o'clock.'

It is ten to. 'Fine,' I say. 'We'll have a drink in the bar.' I escort my mob past the lounge lizards and their stick-insect women who loll back in their chairs and act as if they have never seen small people before.

The waiter makes animated conversation with a nest of them. He pretends we don't exist. I march up to the bar so he can't ignore me. He takes the order for gin and tonic, one coke and an orange juice for the infant.

I find a corner that I hope isn't too discreet and jostle the baby on my knee. She wriggles. She doesn't like it here.

The waiter brings our drinks on an expensive plastic tray and makes a hasty retreat. The nine year old sips his coke elegantly. I don't want to disappoint him. He's been looking forward to this.

I take a large gulp of the gin and tonic. It has as much kick as a snail on a garden path. There is ice in the orange juice. The baby doesn't eat ice. She spits down her front. The lounge lizards look nervous. She doesn't suit their image.

I think about the hours ahead. The woman in purple lamé will make us wait for at least twenty minutes before each course. The baby will squirm on my lap and smear duck sauce all over herself and me, not to mention the tablecloth. I can't help thinking it deserves to have sauce smeared over it. So does the crimson wallpaper and polished floor. And the woman in purple lamé.

But the baby will get tired and bad tempered. I will be on the brink of breakdown and the purple woman will claim victory.

'I've decided to cancel.'

The woman looks startled, but not disappointed. I ask for the drink bill. It's horrendous, as expected. As we head for the door, she says thankyouverymuch. I am unable to reciprocate.

It's often possible to find children in extremely grown-up-looking restaurants. I saw a couple of them the other night.

I caught only a fleeting glimpse of him in the mirror by our table. But he was obviously a monster.

'I'll tell you what you're having,' he boomed at his female companion. 'The soup and the steak.'

I shot my husband a look that said the man deserved to be hanged. My husband didn't disagree. I tried to block out every word the monster said, but my ears were working separately. They fixed attention on him to soak up the next gross remark.

'Hmm, shame they haven't got the turkey,' he said. 'That's what they recommended in the magazine.'

So that's how he'd got here. A magazine had told him where to eat. Now he was frustrated because he couldn't order the food the magazine had told him to eat. I peered briefly into the mirror to get a closer look at him. The features were pointed, the face slightly flushed. The dust-coloured hair hung over a pair of black-rimmed spectacles. A corduroy jacket.

If I'd met him on the street, I'd have assumed he was harmless. Proof of how deceptive first impressions can be. The waiter, younger than even a traffic cop, glided over to their table.

'She's having the soup and the steak and I'll have the soup and the seafood — how do you say it?'

'Quenelles,' the waiter replied.

'What?'

'Quenelles.'

I wondered how on earth his partner contained herself. Perhaps she was his mother and was secretly proud of his oafishness. The waiter disappeared and a female voice struck up sharper and more grating than sand on glass.

'Just two things,' she said in a tone that would have done justice to Catherine the Great. 'Never apologise for being late and *never* ask a waiter how to pronounce something.'

'But why?' he said, unfazed. I sensed her rearing up in her seat.

'Why should a waiter know how to pronounce a word any better than you?'

'Because he's saying it all the time,' he said. 'What do you want me to do — make it up?'

'Anything.'

Any moment now, the cutlery, crockery and possibly the table would start flying. A sudden movement behind me. I ducked. But he was just standing up.

'Where is it?' he asked the waiter.

'Down the back and second on the left.'

Crowded restaurants may be picturesque, fashionable and profitable. But it's somewhat disturbing to be jammed up against a major domestic row. I spoke extra-politely to my husband, who was beginning to look nervous. We ordered champagne and cringed when the man returned.

'All over now?' she said in a tone Victorian nannies used for potty training. 'Or are we going to make an issue of it all night?'

He sat down. She ordered the wine — red and Australian. After the waiter opened the bottle, he poured a small amount into the man's glass for tasting. The man was now terrified of the waiter.

'Is it any good?' he asked the waiter.

'It'll get better.'

By now, the woman's irritation would be building up like the insides of a volcano.

'When?' the man asked.

'After the second glass.'

The waiter vanished — gratefully.

'Now you're wishing I was more sophisticated,' the man said to his woman.

'Am I?' she said, snake-like. 'Are you?'

'Of course I do! I mean, I couldn't come in here wearing gumboots . . . '

'Ah, here's our main course . . . Now, how do you pronounce your dish?'

He spluttered.

'Come on, now. You asked the waiter, not once, but two times. You must know how to say it by now.'

I imagined her looming over him with a whip, ready to lash him with public humiliation. This was dreadful, but she wouldn't stop.

'I have to put up with your stench, your breath, your addiction . . . now this!' she screeched.

I'd been wrong. It wasn't he, but she who was the ogre. But any normal human would have murdered her by now. He had to be a little odd, too.

'That's not bad,' he said with an amused laugh. 'I love you.'

'I'll never leave you,' she said in an earnest low voice.

'Neither will I.'

'Yes, but you have. Three times in five years.'
'But you tell me never to come back.'
'I just curl up and wait for you to knock on the door.'
'Let's skip the pudding,' he said. 'Let's go home.'
They scrambled out the door, barely able to resist tearing each other's clothes off.

Childishness can also come to the fore when people go out in groups. Like the time we went out with Jack and Joan and Graeme and Bev. We were a pretty sight sitting around the table. If Rembrandt had walked past, he wouldn't have been able to resist picking up his paintbrush. Jack and Joan seemed so strong and prosperous in the candlelight. Across from them, Graeme leaned on one elbow with a supernatural glow. Bev sat primly at his side.

'Let me pay,' Jack said when the waitress appeared with the bill lying like a small seagull on her tray.

'No, I insist,' my husband said, choking on his coffee in an uncharacteristic attempt to flourish his chequebook.

Graeme said nothing, but smiled at the exit sign.

'Go on!' Bev said, prodding him in the ribs.

'Why should I?' he said. 'You earn almost as much as I do.'

An unpleasant sensation washed around the table and left each face set.

'But it was our idea,' Joan said with a diplomatic smile as she ground her cigarette into the ashtray.

'Why not go dutch?' I said.

'What, split the bill six ways?' Graeme said, casting an evil eye at Bev.

'Right! That's it,' she snarled, springing up and drawing back her chair as a potential weapon. 'I bear his kids, wash his socks and now he wants me to pay for the meals as well!'

'Sit down, dear,' Joan said calmly. 'There has to be a mature solution to this.'

'Shall I order another bottle while we're at it?' said Jack.

It seemed a good idea, but it wasn't long before all eyes were on the crisp white paper which lay untouched on the tray.

'I don't think we should go dutch,' Joan said as she pinched the tablecloth into tiny ranges. 'Because we asked you out to pay you back for the dinners we've had at your places.'

'But I thought it was our turn?' Bev said blankly.

'No,' said Joan. 'You had us about three weeks ago, remember?'

'But that was only a few drinks!'

'That's not the point,' Jack said. 'At least, that's how we see it, isn't it, darling?'

Joan nodded generously. I cast back desperately trying to recall if Joan and Jack really did owe us. Yes, they had been over for a meal about two months ago — or was it three? But since then, our kids had been to a birthday party there, and what about the drinks they'd given us when we dropped in one afternoon?

'It's been a lovely evening,' I said. 'I really think we should split it three ways.'

'What, among the women?' Graeme sniped. He then winced as if something had attacked him under the table.

'Surely we should pay more than a third?' Bev said. 'We had four courses and you only had three.'

'But we drank more wine.'

'Look here, I really insist,' Jack said, picking up a corner of the bill and shooting an eye at the pen marks. 'On the other hand . . . '

'Let us pay for the wine,' I said.

'Yes, and we'll do the food,' Bev said.

'But where does that leave us?' Joan asked.

'A lot better off!' Graeme laughed loudly.

Maybe Rembrandt wouldn't have liked us so much after all. Not unless he wanted to do a picture of six cave people snarling over a carcase.

'No, this one really is on me,' Jack sighed, reaching for the bill.

But the tray was empty. Graeme the Mean smiled mysteriously.

'Too late,' he said. 'I fixed it.'

4

Mandiddle

THE NINE year old had a friend to stay. Male, of course. Boys that age can never do anything tidily. When they decided to make model aeroplanes, the place ended up looking like Pearl Harbour after the Japanese hit town.

The dining table was covered with planes. Paintbrushes lay about like unexploded missiles in the kitchen. Yoghurt pots full of turps waited like mines for me to trip over. The toddler, naturally, was fascinated.

'Keep *her* out of it!' they said, tearing up the newspaper I hadn't read yet to finish a papier mâché landscape.

'How can I? It's all over the place,' I said. 'If you want her out of the way, you'll have to do that in your room.'

'Okay!' he bellowed, bundling up a tiny percentage of the wreckage. 'C'mon! Let's go!'

His biddable friend gathered up a few more planes and paintbrushes and they marched haughtily off to the bedroom. They left the papier mâché behind to dry. It was beautifully painted. Even the twisting blue river had muddy brown banks.

The toddler was half a step behind them, her white–yellow hair out in spikes and her eyes ablaze with anticipation.

'Stay out!' he said, slamming the door in her face.

She had every reason to burst into tears. I prepared to comfort her with cuddles and playdough. Instead, she did a remarkable thing. She gazed unblinkingly at the door which from her level would have looked like the gates of Windsor Castle and did the toddler equivalent of a shrug. She trudged off to her basket full of books behind the sofa and muttered 'Mandiddle!' under her breath.

It seemed incredible that at the age of two she was already a feminist philosopher. Not only had she realised the futility of trying to penetrate Boys Only games, she understood how pointless they were likely to be. And she'd invented a word for it.

Females get used to mandiddle long before they're fully grown. A young girl's first love will expect her to kneel at his feet while he sits in an armchair and watches war videos. For the privilege of having a boyfriend, she will listen adoringly while he spouts misinformation about computers, guns and rockets. If he goes away on holiday, he will never write.

But the real hurt comes when she realises he's actually more comfortable and happier in the company of other males who can talk the same nonsense. You can hear mandiddle going on in a pub any day of the week. They grunt about sports, jobs, money or they tell jokes about women that make them laugh. In deepest, darkest mandiddle, they're scared stiff of the complexities of emotional, weeping females who demand they 'talk' to them.

Mandiddle isn't about talk, it's about being — preferably bigger, stronger, richer than anyone else. If, when my daughter grows up, she decides to work in the business world, she'll find mandiddle at its most daunting. Bosses behind desks will probably look at her legs before her qualifications. They might even say she's not worth employing because she will have a baby one day.

Her male superiors will be likely to make important decisions in safe men-only domains like pubs, or even loos, where no woman would dare. Even if she does speak up for herself formally, they're likely to snigger about her breasts after she's left the room.

One female executive I know was almost bursting with outrage the other day. She'd just attended a conference. A third of the audience was female, yet the main speaker spent his time making jokes about the size of penises, getting them up and what happens if you drink too much.

His raucous, bawdy approach may have appealed to some of the men, but excluded at least a third of the audience. The underlying message was 'if you haven't got the equipment, you shouldn't be here'.

New Guinea tribesmen ban women from their villages for several days so they can get on with mandiddle in the privacy of their own huts. Sometimes, I think it would be simpler if our own men did the same thing — providing they behaved normally the rest of the year.

I sighed and went over to help my daughter look at her books behind the sofa. But she wasn't reading *Goldilocks* in the shadowy silence. She had somehow got her hands on the papier mâché model the boys had made with such enthusiasm and expertise — and was ripping it to shreds.

It's consolation to know I haven't produced a female wimp. But no matter how hard I try to give her the perfect upbringing, I'm bound to offend someone.

The woman in the feminist bookshop smiled approval. For once, I had been able to bring an infant of the right sex into her domain. Women are terrible about having daughters these days. They're just as bad as the chauvinists who used to demand sons. They will study calendars and douche themselves with all sorts of cooking ingredients in order to conceive the perfect child of the perfect sex. Every pregnant woman seems to crave a female child who will be her friend, confidante and who will go on one day to rule the world.

In this fervour for female offspring, they overlook the fact that mother–daughter relationships are seldom made in heaven. Tinged with jealousies, complexities and thwarted expectations, they're often less successful than mother–son liaisons.

Yet they go on knitting pink booties and 'grieving' loudly in front of their sons for the daughters they should have had. It seems necessary to point out yet again that children are individuals, each with miraculous and infuriating contributions to make.

While a daughter is much less likely to end up in gaol for child molestation or other forms of violence, it's hardly worth introducing a form of genetic Nazism to secure your chances of not having to visit a maximum security prison each week.

In the shop I introduced my daughter to the nonsexist nonracist story books, which are just as self-conscious and dull as ever. We gazed at the poster that says behind every great woman is a man holding her back. There was also a picture of a man pushing a pram.

The pottery, untouched by male hands, was quite nice. I bought a bowl for a friend who would appreciate the female symbol, which somehow isn't as respectable as it used to be.

The woman with the pierced nose and crew cut wrapped the bowl in newspaper. She seemed to be sneering. It was as if she knew what I was going to do next. I hate to say it, but it was by sheer accident we'd parked outside the feminist bookshop. We really were on our way to the corner toyshop — to buy a pram.

As I steered her away from the explicit lesbian lovemaking section, the horror and degradation of such a toy was beginning to sink in. The two year old hadn't asked for one, or even expressed an interest in dolls. But I had decided she was a victim of reverse conditioning. I had steered her so firmly away from traditional female roles that I'd smothered her maternal instincts and possibly had done myself out of the prospect of becoming a grandmother.

So far, her nurturing emotions had been directed only at the cat. It had suffered patiently as she had dragged it by the tail, nearly thrown it in the fire and put its two back legs in the bath. A wartime prison officer couldn't have done much better.

A pram, I thought, might soften her approach. After all, our sons were given trucks and dolls when they were small. She was entitled. I couldn't meet the bookshop feminist's eye. Instead, I studied her corduroy trousers and elastic-sided boots. She grunted pleasure at my daughter clattering in the cardboard carton full of grubby blocks.

I grabbed the child's hand and dragged her to the toyshop. The prams seemed to leave her cold, but I had made my mind up. We prised a man from out the back and demanded the yellow cane pram from the front window.

He blew the dust off its faded colour and offered to wipe the quilted satin lining with a cloth. Not a big demand for prams these days. My daughter seemed to want a new car seat instead.

'Not much point in wrapping it,' said the man.

I supposed he was right. Some things in life aren't easy. One of the most difficult feats is to walk past a feminist bookshop, trying to hide a pram under one arm and carrying a toddler who's bellowing for a car seat under the other.

I didn't dare look as I slung the offensive toy into the station wagon, but I know she was there, pressing her nose against the bookshop window, slitting her eyes and uttering a curse.

To say the pram has been a success would be too fulsome. The cat refused free transportation. Teddies were unresponsive passengers. But I'm pleased to say the pram has found a role — not as a carrier of maternal hopes and dreams, but of books. She stacks them in till the cane sides are bulging, and wheels it around the house with a broad, satisfied smile. I think she's going to be a librarian.

Although it's important to be able to see the amusing side of earnest issues such as feminism, there are still many important issues women must face. Since the feminist revolution of the 70s women no longer expect men to protect them physically and financially.

But few people expected the backlash against women would be so strong. Horrific crimes against women and girls have increased dramatically. There's no doubt that women need protection from such attacks. This time the law must step in and ban video nasties and the violent films that so often provide the blueprint for appalling crimes.

Those who are against censorship of any kind say that there is no link between screen images and people's behaviour afterwards. They conveniently forget that advertisers the world over have long been aware of an audience's susceptibilities. Manufacturers are prepared to fork out millions to have their products aired on screen because they know the influence of the movie camera sinks much further than skin deep.

I went to a preview of a movie called *Blue Velvet* largely because it was an excuse for a night out. I'd heard it was a cult film in the States and there had been disagreement among critics about whether it was great art or nonsense.

It was a small town horror story and, seeing the title was reminiscent of race horses, I didn't think it could be too ghastly. I was wrong. Apart from being violent beyond the point of disgusting (towards the end we were treated to the sight of a dead man's brains oozing from his head), it's the most woman-hating film I've ever seen.

I've always avoided films that are notorious for violence against women. I wouldn't pay to see a female repeatedly stabbed in the shower as happened in *Psycho*. There are no doubt hundreds of films that are more horrible and hating than *Blue Velvet*.

It stars a nightclub singer who sings *Blue Velvet* so badly it's camp and amusing. A maniac drug king has stolen her husband and child in order to have his way with her. A young man finds a mouldering ear in a field. Somehow, he ends up hiding in a wardrobe watching the singer being raped by her repulsive captor.

The drug king produces scissors from his pocket, snips them in the air around her terrified face, then gives the impression he is plunging the scissors into her vagina. We later learn he was only cutting a square from her dressing gown to take with him as a souvenir.

If there's any excuse for portraying such violence, I would like to hear it. But worse was to come. As the movie progresses, we find the helpless little jazz singer is desperate for affection — particularly from the young man who has now emerged from the wardrobe.

She soon makes it apparent the only way she can get pleasure is by being hit. At first, the young man refuses to wallop her. After a while, the poor lad weakens and whacks her one across the face. The force is enough to knock her backwards onto the bed.

We see a smile of satisfaction settle on her lips. Special effects are used to bathe the two figures in a glow, as if their union is more warm and comforting than lying in front of a fire.

It was one of the most dangerous, horrific messages I've seen in a film. It said women love to be beaten, thumped and terrified. If we scream or seem distressed, it's simply because we haven't been treated brutally enough.

Blue Velvet may be a cult film for highly sophisticated people, but an awful lot of young idiots will see it, too. Specially when they hear it's 'explicit'.

The bulk of young people believe what they see on the screen. Their perceptions are formed and their fantasies come alive there. We can hardly be surprised when they act out the scenes they have witnessed.

Several women in the audience walked out. For some reason, I sat on in disbelief, hoping there was sense to be made of it all.

There is an Other Woman in the film. She's pure, blonde, and doesn't go beyond heavy petting. She ends up with her man (the one in the wardrobe), of course. The jazz singer (after having appeared naked and tortured in her lover's garden) ends up sitting on a park bench staring wistfully at the sky.

While I appreciate much of the movie was supposed to be sending up the naive films of the 50s, the violence was nauseating and unforgivable. When the lights went up after the credits, I was astonished that two well-regarded male critics were beaming with delight. They thought *Blue Velvet* was great. Each had a female partner on his arm, who nodded submissive approval. I felt overwhelmed with despair.

A group of women had arranged to meet for a meal after the show. None of us felt like eating. *Blue Velvet* had demonstrated the gulf between the sexes is as wide and as frightening as ever.

5

How do you spell libido, Mum?

I FOUND it scrunched up in his school bag. A postcard of a luscious woman posing semi-naked on a crimson couch. The postcard had been lying around the house for years. Someone had sent it from a gallery in Europe.

It wasn't good enough to treasure, but it was too nice to throw out. So it had spent a lot of time neglected in the back of a drawer. It wasn't great art, but I was delighted that he'd liked it enough to carry around with him. I was about to tell him so when I saw his face was pink with embarrassment.

'We look at them at school,' he said sheepishly.

'Oh, are you studying art history?'

'No. Women without any clothes on.'

'During lessons?' I said, still thinking of the art department.

'At lunchtime.'

'Oh.'

My heart sank. He was only nine. Was he ready to join a clan of leering, pimple-speckled louts already? Childhood these days is so short, it's almost non-existent.

'All the other kids take *Playboy* and *Penthouse*.'

'Where do they get them from?'

'Home, of course.'

All of a sudden, I saw the staidly married parents of his friends in a new light. Did they really keep stacks of titillating magazines under the bed? Apart from the fact I'd always associated *Playboy* and *Penthouse* with passion-starved bachelors, I was amazed anyone could still afford the magazines.

I wondered how the plump Victorian model stood up against her modern counterparts with their racehorse thighs and gynaecological poses. Somehow or other, it seemed she had passed — out of freak value, perhaps. Proof that women have had the same number of everything for centuries.

'Haven't we got anything better?' he said, snatching the postcard from my hand.

There was the Bonnard in the bedroom, but she was modestly concealed by a towel. It's an impression of sensuality that to me is much more effective than a touched-up shot of a nineteen year old with silicone boobs. I doubted he'd understand. Besides, it would never fit in his school bag.

Not for the first time, I experienced the liberal parent's dilemma. Should I casually offer to buy him a soft-core magazine in the hope he'd get it out of his system?

It might make us friends for life. He'd experience an adolescence free of hang-ups. There would be no shame-filled attempts to conceal sheets and underclothes. He'd tell me everything — even about his girlfriends.

Or would it simply fuel the fire and result in a huge explosion when some nosy-parker teacher caught them at It? Whatever It was, I assumed it had to be harmless. At that age.

And what about exploitation of women? Surely I shouldn't encourage him to see those poor pin-up girls as objects? He might automatically become the sort of man whose eye you can't meet. A man who lurks around massage parlours with his hands in his pockets. Someone who tries to pick up women at bus stops and swimming pools.

I cast myself back to the time I was nine. Sex was like a giant blister looming on the horizon, but nobody talked about it. Nobody half-decent, that is.

I later learned it was the only conversation topic that made adults shut up with silly smiles on their faces when I walked in the room. I'd always imagined they'd been talking about something more serious and monumental. Like the future of the universe. Or me.

But that was back in the old days when kids really were innocent. Now, thanks to television, they know all about everything. From AIDS to suicide. He's bound to have encyclopaedic knowledge about contraception and abortion, too. I never like to ask him — not so much out of prudishness, but more because he's bound to find out too soon, anyway.

'What do you do with these pictures?' I asked.

'We look at them,' he giggled helplessly.

How do you spell libido, Mum?

That night, he had a serious talk with his father.

'What did he say?' I asked my husband afterwards.

'He says they're like you, but different.'

I was beginning not to cope. It seemed like just a few weeks ago that he was a baby lying in my arms with a hospital tag around his neck. Sometime between then and now, he'd turned into a knowing old man. Any moment now, he'd be bringing home a pregnant girlfriend.

Next day, when he came home from school, I quizzed him closely, but not too intensely.

'How did it go at lunchtime?' I said casually.

'Great.'

'Great?'

'Yeah, we played on skateboards.'

It wasn't long after that he found the Real Thing. I know love is supposed to be an up and down affair, but this is ridiculous. The trampoline was a last ditch attempt to wean him off television. The box was an addiction. He'd trudge home from school, shut himself in his room and plug in for his daily fix.

There are some advantages in rearing a television junkie. You don't have to talk to him for a start, and you don't have to find him anything else to do. If he emerges with an irritating request or observation, you can shoo him back in to worship at the shrine of materialism.

After a few years, however, despair sets in. The astonishing stresses of parenthood aren't worth enduring for a blob who knows more about The Golden Girls than you. There's also the matter of fitness. Remember how kids used to run in the old days? They'd walk miles without the slightest complaint. They were healthy because television and junk food hadn't been invented and only doctors had cars.

I hoped the trampoline would help him discover his legs. But when I bullied him away from Dr Who and made him clamber onto the thing, he wasn't that keen. He bobbed up and down a few times and staggered off clutching his chest. I wondered if heart surgeons took plastic cards.

The trampoline stood out there by the back hedge week after week. Apart from providing a sunbathing spot for the cat and a place for grass to grow yellow underneath, it seemed to have no purpose. It hadn't been cheap. I was on the verge of trading it in for a recliner rocker for my premature geriatric, when a strange thing happened.

I woke one Saturday to find him springing up and down on the thing like a Russian gymnast. Higher and higher he soared. He looked quite graceful, apart from the fact his feet were sticking out like a duck's and his neck was swivelled sideways.

'That's lovely, darling,' I said. 'Only, point your toes and you're supposed to look straight ahead.'

The advice fell on ears that chose to hear no better than a stone. But the enthusiasm seemed to grow hour by hour. The crooked neck was probably hereditary. From his side. The kid made the exercise look so appealing that I decided to have a go when he'd shot off to the loo. On my way toward the clouds, I spied another trampoline in the back yard over the hedge. On it bounced two long-haired girls — the sort that picture books are made of. They pretended not to see me, so I returned the compliment. So that's what had caused the neck problem.

Next morning, the hedge was mutilated to half its size. A dart sailed through the sky and landed in the cabbages.

'They want to know my name!' he said breathlessly.

He scrawled a reply, sent it back and bounced in anticipation.

'You can't spell very well,' said a face that suddenly appeared over the top of the hedge.

He stopped and turned the colour of a summer rose.

'How did you get there?'

'I'm on a ladder, so don't touch me or I'll fall off.'

She watched, critical, as he leapt about.

'Can't you go any higher than that?'

Already on the point of going into orbit, he heaved his knees up to his chest and set his arms whirling like a pair of propellers. I had given birth to the world's first flying man.

So this is how it feels to be the mother of the bridegroom. You spend years of your life coughing up for space invaders and model paint. You know his faults and failures with greater intimacy than the fast-breeding wrinkles on your face. Then some smart upstart in a pastel pinafore turns up and kicks him around. And he takes notice.

'What's your mother doing?'

'Sunbathing. Mum, sit up properly!'

How do you spell libido, Mum?

I rolled onto my stomach and watched the helpless slave jump higher, harder, faster. The fool was enjoying it. Couldn't he see she was a heartbreaker?

'Point your toes!' she snapped at him.

He drew a breath and started cavorting about like Nureyev in his heyday. As I tried to shove my body into an acceptable shape, I wondered if there were any good kids' programmes on TV.

He'll be ten tomorrow. A whole decade. To say a kid is special is like saying it gets dark at night. I'm going to do it anyway. He turned up by accident, the way many babies do. It took a while to get used to the idea. I already had a toddler demanding every second of the day. I had no idea how I'd cope when the bulge in my stomach materialised into another human.

I fell in love the moment I clapped eyes on him. He was a startled pixie, nervous of the world. I soon learned he'd calm down if I snuggled him in my dressing gown and stroked his back.

Even in those days, he was intense about life. He'd stare up at the beamed ceiling in the living room till he was cross-eyed. Maybe it was guts ache.

I was surprised how gentle his two-year-old brother was with him. The little one admired his brother like mad. As the younger one grew into toddlerhood, they developed a relationship that involved daily shouting matches over toys, who said what when, and all the other stuff. It was natural, seeing they bathed, slept, ate and played together.

To tell the truth, they were exhausting. Sometimes, I felt like a charioteer with two horses running in different directions. But the underlying feeling was very loving and strong.

I worried about the little one when he got asthma. Was he so much in his brother's shadow he needed illness for attention? The thought made me squeeze up with anxiety as he lay in the doctor's surgery with the green plastic mask over his face and when I listened to his barking cough at night, waiting for it to get worse.

He was a battler, even then. After two years, the asthma had cleared and it was time to start school. I hated those first few days at home without him. It was reassuring to know his brother would take him under his wing in the playground jungle — and he did.

Sometimes they'd come home together. Other days, they'd

trudge home separately after a monumental row.

It's impossible to say some things softly, to wrap them up in fairy floss so they sound nice. One day, those two kids went down the road. Only one of them, the little one, came back.

Our family was decimated. It was a dreadful, harsh time for us. Sometimes, I looked at my younger son — and wondered how he'd cope. At the delicate age of six he had seen his brother mown down on the road.

I assumed it would mean not one, but two tragedies. The six year old would be haunted by nightmares, bed wetting and other unimaginable problems for years. No way would he have a healthy childhood, I thought.

There were nightmares to start with — monsters in cars chasing him. School work wasn't too hot that year, either. But as time passed, I was amazed to see him laugh again. With incredible courage, he worked at finding friends and keeping them. He had every right to crumple up in a corner and say he was the unluckiest boy in the world. He never did.

On the days I felt I couldn't endure the sadness any more, I'd see his determination to survive — and be ashamed of my self-indulgence.

Now he's nearly ten, I'm often amazed by his breadth of understanding. He knows about pain, and about coming out the other side. I guess it's a lesson we all have to learn — later rather that sooner, given the choice.

Instead of turning into a wreck, it seems he has special things to offer because he's been through so much. I'm amazed and grateful. He's sprouting skyward now. My startled pixie has grown quite handsome. Half-friends, half-lovers, our relationship is entering that twilight zone. He used to be proud to be seen with me. Now I feel proud being with him.

We cross the road — always cautiously — to a steak and chips joint. We wrist wrestle on the table, till he sets the vinegar bottle nearly flying.

'I like it here,' he says, shovelling chips in his mouth. 'It's not Italian and it's not Chinese.'

Afterwards, he swaggers out to the kitchen to tell the chef it's the best meal he's had for ages. The chef, a cigarette wedged between his lips, nods appreciation.

The windscreen wipers slap as we drive back home in the dark.

How do you spell libido, Mum?

I pray he's seen the worst life can dish out.   From now on, it's got
to be good.
   'I love you,' he says.
   My night is complete.

6

Designer dads

I SAW my father again the other night. It wasn't a ghostly spectre standing at the end of the bed. It was much warmer and more real than that. My son and I were out for the evening with a family of friends. We went back to their place afterwards for wine, cheese and chippies. You can never count on elegance when there are kids around. Even before we sat down, the bawdy jokes began.

Their mother and I shared smiles of relief when the level was raised to Monty Python stories. Her 12 year old and my son knew all the accents and innuendoes by heart — the exploding bushes, the joke that makes people die laughing and the grannies who beat up thugs.

Oddly enough, that's when I saw Dad sitting at the end of the table. His face was bubbling with humour and his hands waved expansively at the end of each phrase.

Genetics is a funny business. It's less about engineering and more to do with a massive lucky dip of chromosomes. You end up with your mother's chin, you father's ear and your great aunt's eyebrow. Even if you thought your nose was your own design, you're likely to find it jutting out at you from a Victorian photo album that used to belong to your grandmother.

Physical characteristics aren't the only things you pick up in the family lucky dip. I've known people who have their uncle's cynical wit and their grandmother's fear of open spaces combined with their father's tendency to sulk. The mixture can seem bizarre, but it's often quite recognisable if you know the person's family well enough.

Dad has been dead three years now but he was very much alive that night in my son. The fiery blue eyes brimming with delight at telling a good story; the enthusiastic reach for another handful of chips while someone else had his turn.

Designer dads

Dad never was a Monty Python fan, but the stories that night could just as easily have been about the time he fell off a tram when he was twenty-three, or about how he discovered Japanese massage. I'd sat around many tables like this before with that sensation of listening with fondness while the plot unravelled.

There's no doubt that my son is his own person. There are parts of him I don't recognise, and sometimes find hard to understand. But his links with Dad have been there since the day he was born. It was strange to find a newborn baby with hands exactly like his grandfather's. They could both stretch their fingers backwards in a curve like Indonesian dancers.

Dad is in the toddler, too. Sometimes, when she stops and lies on the floor to dream for a while, I know she's off on one of his imagination flights, seeing the world through the eyes of a giant, or maybe a housefly.

When people die, you never lose them completely. They become part of you. During their lifetime they weave things into your makeup that can never be taken out.

He's still around in other ways, too. When I visited my mother a few days ago, I knew I'd have to look in Dad's shed. He never spent a lot of time in there, the way some men live in their sheds. But it's still very much his territory, a space no one else has invaded.

He kept it fairly tidy in the last years of his life. It was as if he knew he might die sometime soon, so he fitted the hammers and screwdrivers into size-graded braces on the wall, and kept the benchtop neat and orderly.

Most of his stuff, the rakes and pitchforks that have been around since before I was born, is still there in the cool, musty silence.

My brother is forty now, but his old surfboard is up in the rafters, waiting for him to shed his years like skin, slap on Coppertone and his old 'baggies' to ride the waves again.

A faded cane doll's crib stands on crippled legs. It's full of wire now. The first time I saw the thing it was lavishly decorated in pink frills — a wonderful gift for a four year old who was going to have her tonsils out.

It's here that Dad made a doll's house and a soldiers' castle for his grandchildren, and concocted evil potions to destroy leaf curl. He's still here among the dusty fizzy drink bottles, spider-webbed watering can and rusty tool boxes.

Clouds of happiness

There are many things I'd like to share with him now. Family occasions have a hollow centre because he's not there any more. But when I see my son tell a really good joke with an ending that's so good he can hardly wait to reach it, I know that Dad isn't far away at all.

If there's one word that sums up this decade, it's pressure. Everyone seems to have more of it to cope with than before. There was a time when all a man had to do was to wave politely at his offspring through the hospital glass and he was considered a decent father. These days, a dad has to be so much more.

Superdad was born in the last decade. He's a warm and wonderful person who not only remembers his kids' names, but takes them for walks and changes their nappies, too.

You see him out at weekends pushing a pram with one hand and trailing a toddler with the other. Not since Biblical times have there been so many saintly faces on the streets.

Superdad started about the time male guilt set in. After the feminists had finally driven their point home, some men began to realise they had been monsters and it was time to change.

They read the right books and realised it was immoral to forbid their wives from working. The pill ensured that every child — well, almost every child — was wanted. It became compulsory for Dad, no matter how squeamish, to attend the birth.

A man cannot be a Superdad unless he breathes through every contraction, pants when the baby's head crowns and buries the placenta under a bush in the garden. He must laugh, cry and read with his children, wash their clothes and whip up marvellous chicken casseroles in between times. In short, he must be everything his own father wasn't. He's loving, caring and physically demonstrative towards his children.

Superdads are wonderful, but they shouldn't have too big a fuss made over them. After all, they are only doing what fathers should have been at for centuries.

Kids need to grow up knowing both parents. Dad shouldn't be a shadowy figure who lurks behind the newspaper at breakfast and slinks off to the pub at night. Such a creature deserves nothing more than the socks, ties and underarm deodorant the advertisers say he should get on Father's Day.

For every Superdad, there are several thousand who haven't

made it. A newly released book I've found shows just how far dads have to go. This collection of children's perceptions of their dads has a chilling undertone.

'A dad is best at sleeping, thinking, saying maybe or one day and eating,' writes Anna, aged nine.

Who needs to read fairy tales about the selfish giant when he's alive and well?

'I love my dad because he has lots of Christmas parties to go to at Christmas time,' says Shannon, aged eight.

Is this because Christmas parties ensure Dad is safely out of the house for a guaranteed period? Or does the booze make Dad cheerful and loosen his inhibitions enough to make him slightly affectionate?

The quotes are amusing, but, at the same time, some of them portray a bleak domestic landscape with Dad as a distant, almost sinister, figure.

'My dad is best at killing Mum's plants with the lawnmower,' writes Amber, aged nine.

It's hardly surprising that mums all over the country have taken to booting these unpleasant-sounding oafs out of their homes altogether. The slave is free of her lazy, demanding oppressor and the kids can't miss a dad they never knew.

It isn't till the oaf–dad throws his suitcase on the single wirewove in the dingy bedsit that he might begin to think. He might remember the birthday parties he couldn't make because of rugby practice, the stories he was always going to read 'later' and the camping trip they were going to have 'one day'.

Sometimes, the oaf–dad tries to change. He gives the kids great outings when he has custody at weekends. He starts to learn to listen and cuddle. He might even begin to see their mother as an individual with her own needs and aspirations. He lets her know what a great dad he can be.

The rejected oaf–dad has every reason to be heartbroken. He didn't realise how precious his family was when he had it. Now he wants it back more than anything else on earth. But it's usually too late.

No matter how irritating the dad in your house can be sometimes, you have to admit it could be much worse. For example, living with Herb Alpert must be a major nightmare. Who could stand him practising Tijuana Taxi in the garage all night? He also looks suspiciously like a man who wears the type of hair oil that makes pillowcases look as if you've been frying eggs on them.

There are other appalling prospects, too. People like:

- Dennis Thatcher: He'd demand to be dominated all the time. You'd get exhausted being a 24-hour iron maiden. Men on two legs are more fun.
- Prince Charles: Who could live with a man who collects toilets for a hobby?
- Ronald Reagan: Looks like a snorer and plays with war toys.
- Someone who builds a yacht in the front garden: Men who do this are really fantasising about leaving home. They don't have the nerve to say it outright, so they build a monument to disappearance where everyone can see it.

   As it happens, they might as well leave because they spend every spare moment out there glueing bits of wood together. They never take less than ten years to build the thing. If they ever get it finished, they decide they've 'grown out' of boats and take up squash.

   The boat is always bigger than expected, due to a metric confusion, and it won't get out of the gate. It has to be taken by helicopter to the local tip.
- An evangelist: Even though these characters tend to be incredibly and inexplicably wealthy, one of them would be really hard to take. He would believe in corporal punishment and the bomb. And he'd practise in front of the mirror every night.
- Any sort of football player: He'd produce mountains of smelly socks, and you'd never be able to make roast potatoes like his mum did.
- Danny La Rue: It's difficult enough keeping track of your own earrings without your husband swiping them.
- Napoleon: Anyone who, on his way back from battle, sends his wife the message 'Don't wash' has got to be interesting. Great for parties, but too short.
- John Cleese: Too tall.
- Shakespeare: Delightfully literate, but too old.
- Michael Jackson: How can you be faithful to a man who keeps changing his looks? You could hop into bed with the window washer by mistake.

Designer dads

- Fish and chip shop proprietors: Their wives always look miserable.
- Sir Winston Churchill: Cigars are out.
- Salvador Dali: So are clocks that melt.
- A handyman: Guaranteed to reduce your house to ruins.
- A ladies' man: Certain to dislike and fear women under all that aftershave. Probably gay.
- Someone who plays golf: The game isn't so bad, but the hats and T-shirts are terrible.
- Peter Pan: A lost boy who is always needing time out to find himself. Better off to hire a nanny for him.

Maybe sometimes it pays to be grateful none of these men walked, crawled, sailed or flew into your life. Most of us have enough problems already.

7

Beached

THERE'S NOTHING like a day at the beach. It's one of the most relaxing things you can do after a hard week's work. It's simply a matter of getting out of bed soon after sunrise to pack bags full of togs, towels, tan lotion, insect repellent, hats, bibs, a full change of clothes, napkins for the baby and sandwiches.

'Did you remember the fruit drinks?' I say as we hit the rugged countryside halfway between city and beach.

'No. Did you? There's bound to be a shop when we get there.'

There isn't. Instead, we meet a traffic cop standing in the bend of the road where the shop should be. He can tell we're a meek family group who is unlikely to pull a sawn-off shotgun on him, so he's fairly cocky: 67 kilometres per hour in a 50 kilometres per hour area. We can see it on his machine if we like. No, thanks.

'What's your excuse, madam?' he says.

I could tell him I'm already strung up about spending the day at the beach.

'I didn't see the sign,' I say.

'It's right behind you.'

'And my speedometer's not working.'

'Someone else has said that already today,' he says, tearing a leaf off his pad.

With the feeling a fish must get when it realises the hook is stuck irrevocably in its cheek, I know I'm caught. A large instant fine, and the baby is bound to get dehydrated.

The beach is covered with sparkling black sand designed to fry the soles off your feet. I set out with the bravado of a firewalker, chillybin on one arm, baby on the other. It's amazing the number of things the mothers of small children learn to do with one hand. Heating up milk, filling a bottle and screwing the lid on is one feat, talking on the telephone and taking a message is another. I've

Beached

been known to cook a batch of muffins, vacuum an entire house and ice a cake with one hand. Peeling potatoes is more of a challenge. With enough practice, I could probably play a Beethoven sonata with a child crooked under my left arm.

'Where are my thongs?' the ten year old wails as if I'm personally responsible for setting the sand alight.

Everyone else has brought beach umbrellas. They gaze smugly out to sea from the shade. I never thought to pack one.

Choosing a spot isn't easy. We can't sit by the raging shoreline. Apart from the fact the baby will run into the water all the time, we'd be in danger of getting swamped. The middle of the beach is so full of umbrellas, it looks like a mushroom paddock. We, the underprivileged species in the ecosystem, have to scramble up the bank to perch in the marram grass.

One of the great rules of the beach is that babies must wear hats. Otherwise they'll get burnt. The baby refuses to wear hers. It sits on her scalp like a pink pancake for a matter of seconds before she hauls the elastic under her chin up to rest moustache-like under her nose. She then tugs it off so the whole hat rests under her chin like a feeding bag.

The ten year old and his father gallop off into the furious waves. Further out, boys on their boards are having a great time daring fate to do its worst.

Life is often like a beach. You bob up and down waiting to catch the waves. All the people around you seem able to hop on their waves at just the right times, and ride victoriously in to shore.

You, on the other hand, spend most of your time heaving yourself onto waves that aren't ripe yet. They slip past with a cheeky glint so some other so-and-so can get them. When you finally see the Big One swelling up on the horizon, you know it's yours. Every muscle in your body twitches. Just when you've got yourself in the champion-surfer-about-to-lunge position, it explodes into white water and grinds you into the sand.

The baby wants a sandwich. She likes her bread with plenty of sand on it. Of course, no one is supposed to go near water for twenty minutes after they've eaten. She demands to splash in the waves straight away. I follow her down to the shore.

Deeper and deeper she wants to go. But the undercurrent is strong. She tugs my hand and bellows. Passers-by glare in disapproval, certain I've been hitting her again.

'Hey, Mum!' says a ten-year-old sea monster. 'There's blue-bottles and jellyfish!'

'Well, stay away from them and don't go out too deep and put on some more suntan lotion when you come in. You don't want to get skin cancer, do you?'

'You should come in!' his father calls from the sea. 'The water's great!'

I know what will happen if I do. The baby will stand on the shore and yell till I get back.

All of a sudden, the beach has made me terribly tired. A mosquito is chomping at my elbow and something resembling a crab's claw is digging into my toe. The workday week begins to seem like a holiday.

But sometimes, even during the week, you can find magic at a beach when you least expect it . . .

The lunchtime sun had driven everyone out of their offices. They crawled along the street like sweltering cockroaches, clinging to the shade of the buildings.

In an effort to find some cool air, I drove to the beach. I should have known it would be crowded. I missed the first park and drove on. The road was packed with late-model Japanese cars. Even the yellow lines were taken.

I paused at a pedestrian crossing and glanced across at the beach. Immaculately tanned bodies were lined up like frankfurters on the sand. They were all fighting for a tiny patch on which they could find serenity, a breath of wind and the sort of tan advertisements are made of.

The perfume of expensive lotion lay heavy on the air. Designer bikinis, French sunglasses, imitation Italian icecreams and ghetto blasters. Whatever happened to ordinary days at the beach? I couldn't face it. Not in the heat.

I put my foot down on the accelerator and followed the sea wall till traffic thinned out. I parked in an almost deserted spot. It was too hot to stay in the car, so I got out and sat on the wall. It seemed crazy that all those people had squeezed themselves onto that little beach when there was so much space here. But it wasn't conventionally beautiful. The shore was jagged and the icecream shop was just a speck on the horizon.

The sea washed restlessly over the rocks, daring me to touch it. I walked past a group of scruffy people — the sort you don't meet eyes with, just in case — and headed down some grubby steps to the water. I took my shoes off, jammed them in my handbag and bathed my feet in the wonderful waves.

Suddenly, there was a sinister laugh behind me. I turned to see a fierce-looking young woman coming down the steps. She wore cut-off jeans and a torn shirt. Strings of long, black hair hung over her face.

A small child tagged along behind her. He was more carefully dressed, but his legs were covered with sores and flea bites. I tried not to let her know I was alarmed.

'Great day,' she said, letting the waves wash over her feet. She smiled to reveal a mouth almost devoid of teeth. Those that were left were brown with decay. I felt a pang of pity when I saw one of her eyes was purple and swollen. She could have been beautiful — if someone had fixed up her hair and teeth — and that eye.

I was just beginning to relax when a huge male figure appeared at the top of the steps. As he thundered down toward us, a strange tension built up. We all knew they could mug me here. Nobody would see us tucked away below the road. My screams would be drowned by the roar of the sea.

I wished I'd stayed on the other beach safe in so many ways. I stared down at the water and prepared for violent impact. He hesitated, then lunged toward me — no, past me — straight into the waves. Fully clothed. With the grace of a wild animal he heaved himself under the water. We watched his shape slipping away from us.

'I hope he drowns,' she said flatly.

'He's probably trying to impress you,' I said.

'No,' she said. 'He's my brother.'

When he surfaced, huffing and snorting, I saw that he too had a black eye.

'We were in a fight last night,' he said as if he'd read my mind. 'Salt water's good for black eyes.'

It seemed odd that such a fearsome fellow used the same old-fashioned remedies my aunt would recommend.

'Gangs were not involved,' he said, waving a finger at me like a courtroom lawyer. 'It was street kids. They had knives.'

He hurled himself on his back and floated. The child whinged at his mother's side, but she brushed him off and threw herself into the waves, clothes and all. The child stood on the steps and cried. I tried to console him, but he didn't trust me. I looked too much like a social worker.

'Come on in!' the man called to me.

I wanted to drop everything and surrender. Then I remembered my dress. It had cost a fair bit, even if it was in a sale. The salt water would ruin it. And how would I explain it away when the magic was over and I straggled back, wet through, to the car?

'I'm a water baby,' the man said, as if we were having a conversation over a bar. 'I'm a Pisces — that's a water sign. I just can't stick with one woman. I'll only stay so long, then I shoot through. I don't mean it. I can't help it.'

He turned on his stomach and disappeared under the water. I turned and hurried up the steps. I didn't want to say goodbye. When he surfaced into the sun again, everything would still be there, except me. I'm sure he understood.

A while after that, I met another weird character at a beach. He appeared in the distance, looking like some kind of insect. A pair of earphones were clapped over his elongated head.

In one hand, he held a long metal stick which he waved slowly from side to side, as if it was sniffing something buried deep in the sand, or perhaps vacuuming the beach.

He wasn't a lovable creature. His legs were too spindly, the nose too pointed to inspire affection. The midwinter strollers kept clear of him instinctively. The world's scavengers aren't sought after as a rule. Vultures make friends among their own kind, crabs tend to be loners and seagulls don't have a good reputation among polite company.

Yet he seemed to want companionship, if not approval. He was almost grateful when I intercepted his path and asked, stupidly, if he came here often.

'Oh, every day,' he said, gazing enigmatically at the horizon. 'But some of them only come out at night. They're too ashamed to be seen in public.'

'Why, do people say things to you?'

'Oh, no. They never say anything. Just think, "What right have you got to go around picking up stuff other people have dropped?"'

Although he was pleased to talk, he couldn't help whirling the metal detector in tiny circles by his feet and checking the gauge.

'They think you're going to get all these gold rings and watches and trade them in for a fortune,' he said. 'But I don't do it for myself. Well, not always.'

I peered into his sunglasses to see if I could perceive the eyes of a saint. Unfortunately, they were too dark to reveal anything. As we stood there, I got the old Darth Vader feelings back again. Everyone's supposed to hate Darth because he's so mean and evil. But take away his helmet and breathing apparatus and he curls up in a pile of green goo. Under all that armour is a Darth who feels inferior and whose mother potty trained him too soon.

The metal detector man, stripped of his blue peaked cap, sunglasses and equipment, would no doubt be just as helpless.

'I found an engagement ring for a couple once,' he said. 'I just walked along the beach and they said she'd lost it. It was really good to help them out.'

Other metal detector men weren't so pleasant, he explained. Another nice young couple he knew lost a ring at a beach up north. They advertised for a metal detector man and told him which part of the beach to search.

They arranged to meet him, but he never showed up. They reckon he went early, found the ring and took off.

'The thing about women and beaches is their fingers shrink when they get in the cold water,' he said. 'That's why it's always good to look along the shoreline. It's where you find the rings.'

Freak high tides were good, too, because they turned up stuff that had been lost for years. He even found a gold sovereign once.

'It's a hobby, really,' he said, as I followed his compulsive little steps along the shore. 'I mean, it doesn't do anyone any harm. Most of them just claim on insurance, so someone might as well have it.'

When I asked what he did with the watches, rings and bits of money he found, he was vague. Maybe he just kept them in a jar on his dressing table, or gave them to friends and relatives. Neither seemed particularly likely.

Scavengers may acknowledge pathos in their job, but they are essentially creatures of profit. Otherwise, there'd be no point.

'I don't mind going out during daylight,' he said. 'I'm not ashamed. I don't take the detector out on the streets, though. That would be a bit much.'

For the first time, the metal detector man looked at me. There was no gold chain about to slip from my neck, no diamond stud about to tumble from my ears, no perilously large emerald ring.

'S'pose I'd better be going,' he said.

'Good luck,' I said politely.

'They're not cheap, these machines,' he said, mistaking my expression for envy. 'But you can join a club. They go on outings.'

The thought of the beach covered in metal detector men was too much. It would look as if Mars had landed and materialism really had gone mad.

All of a sudden, it was too chilly to stay. I hurried back to the warmth of the station wagon. The metal detector man trudged on.

8

I always thought shares were something to do with sheep

WHEN GREGORY turned up one day and offered to buy some shares for me, it would have been madness to resist. He had, after all, made a fortune on the market. The money seemed an embarrassment to him.

After he'd bought several houses and cars and lots of computer things, he didn't know what to do. So he decided to become a benefactor, which was very nice of him. Instead of being one of the guilty rich, he was offering the opportunity of wealth to his friends and relatives.

Apart from liking Gregory and not wanting to hurt his feelings, I was pretty sure I'd know what to do with a spare few hundred thousand, so I said yes and gave him my life savings.

'Is this all?' he said, staring at the cheque.

'What's wrong with two hundred dollars?' I said. 'It's taken ages to save that amount.'

'Oh, nothing. It's just that sharebrokers don't look at anything less than one thousand dollars.'

'Really?' I said, wondering at the wealth out there.

When there are children to feed and clothe, videos to hire and birthday presents to buy, it's amazing anyone can save one thousand dollars. Maybe they're mostly sippies (single, independent party-going persons) rather than woppies (worn-out penniless parents).

He folded the cheque in half, anyway, and slipped it in his breastpocket. I had great hopes for that two hundred dollars, which was soon to be two thousand dollars and possibly two million.

First, I would put a phone in the bathroom. Friends seem to have automatic bleeper systems that set off the second I step into hot water. A phone by the bath would save a lot of dripping wet conversations and be incredibly luxurious.

Clouds of happiness

A dishwasher would be next, and a stereo with an arm that came back automatically when the record had finished. Then, if I got really rich, I'd hire a muscular masseur to rub me over every morning before I got out of bed.

Gregory seemed to disappear for several months. We did have a telephone conversation in which I managed to ask casually how the two hundred dollars was doing. Great, he said. It was worth half as much again.

A feeling of remorse set in. If only I'd sold the car and given him six thousand dollars, it would be worth nine thousand dollars by now. It really was too late, I supposed, to ask him to hang on a bit and babysit some more cash for me. So I didn't ask.

Anyway, there's something tacky about making millions by producing nothing at all, not even toilet roll holders. Millionaires used to be rare, glamorous creatures. If they weren't interesting, they were at least eccentric and incredibly rich.

Millionaires aren't like that any more. They're everywhere, laying Italian marble on their kitchen floors, scrubbing their yachts and buying property in the Pacific.

Money's not what it used to be. Because of inflation and floating dollars, just about anyone with a bit of dedication can make a million. It doesn't even sound much any more — not compared to the world's population, the number of solar systems in the universe or how many times your calculator can multiply seventy thousand by nine billion. In the larger cities, a quarter of a million will buy only a modestly spacious home.

We mustn't be disappointed when millionaires turn out dreary, twitchy and lacking in conversation. They have devoted their lives to making money, the way saints used to devote their lives to God.

They haven't had time to savour the colours of sunset, study the moods of Beethoven or struggle with a French novel. The only aspect of human nature they know much about is greed — and it doesn't make pleasant chat.

There's a hollow ache inside most of us — a yearning that is anaesthetised only by a new CD player, a rug from Iran or a new computer. Sadly, the ache vanishes only temporarily at the moment of possession. It quickly returns, and the haunted feeling of wanting comes back.

God doesn't seem to work any more. Even physical exercise requires an array of designer tracksuits, running shoes and ten-speeds. The only place families seem happy is on American sitcoms.

I still can't understand why, when the country goes into the red for billions, it's called a respectable national debt. But when I overspend by a few dollars, the bank manager sends shirty letters that question my honour and suggest our relationship is on the rocks.

After one of those letters, Gregory came to a party at our place. When the mood was right, I willed myself to mention (in a terribly relaxed manner) the two hundred dollars.

'Haven't you heard?' Gregory said. 'I lost all my money.'

'What, even the houses?'

'All of them, except I've just managed to hang onto the one we live in.'

'That's terrible! You poor thing! So you haven't got my two hundred dollars any more?'

'Not really. Well, I could scrape around and find you *a* two hundred dollars, but it wouldn't be *your* two hundred dollars.'

'Oh, no,' I said. 'Just you hang onto it.'

It's reassuring to know I'll never suffer the problems of the wealthy. When it became apparent I'd never 'win' a dishwasher on the stock exchange, I decided to get one on credit, like everyone else.

The queue was reminiscent of those old war movies that show refugees lining up for their papers. The atmosphere was joyless. The people scruffy.

Even if you felt okay before you stepped on the worn mustard carpet, the place soon dragged you down. I had unwittingly dressed for the occasion in an old yellow raincoat. My daughter seemed to be bursting out of her purple one and her red tights were rolling slowly toward the floor.

The man in front of us had a frayed square on the rump of his jeans. I didn't turn to look at the woman behind, but the tone of her voice said it all.

'Jason! Brandon! Stop doing that!' she harped at her two sons who were dressed in identical brown parkas. 'Jason! Stop touching it!'

They were fascinated by a depressing little sign that advertised top interest rates in red moving figures. They weren't touching it so much as bouncing around it. She wasn't complaining about their activity so much as their presence on earth and her fatigue.

Vacuum cleaner, I thought. She probably had a recent model at home, but had found some minor fault. She needed a new one with a particular type of computerised dust filter to make life less painful, for a while.

'I came here earlier and all the booths were full,' said the woman in my ear. 'I thought I'd come back later. I had no idea there'd be a queue.'

We clasped our tickets that described what we wanted to buy and gazed morosely at the people already ensconced in booths. They were separated by cheap mahogany veneer and glass patterned in thick little squares.

My daughter picked up the mood of the place. She rolled around on the floor and scratched at a lump of grey chewing gum stuck in the carpet. Tubes of fluorescent lights glared down at her.

Credit isn't a dirty word. Not any more. Specially if it's interest-free for six months.

They make it sound so glamorous on television. It's crazy not to buy an appliance that way. So why was I wishing so fervently I had paid cash for the dishwasher?

The woman in the polo neck didn't beckon us or call us over. She just looked out from her tired green eyes and nodded. There were two plain black seats to choose from in her booth. I took the one closest to her desk and plonked the child on the other.

The woman seemed surprised when I wrote out a cheque for a hefty deposit. She had to check it out with her boss. I guess it had to be expected she would want to know my name, address and phone number, and if we owned the house or if it was rented. We're talking credit, after all.

I didn't mind telling her my job and where I worked. When she asked how long I'd worked there, I began to get on edge. She also wanted to know where I'd worked before this job.

My self-confidence was beginning to weaken when she asked for our previous address. She wasn't happy we'd lived there only six months. She wanted to know where we had lived before that, for how long, and what the phone number was.

Maybe I have problems, but there's no way I can recall a phone number I had two years ago in another city. I stared at a clock with hands stuck at 1.45 and thought about inventing a number. But the consequences could have been disastrous.

By this stage my daughter had decided to take off her gumboots and turn her chair into a climbing frame. She thumped against the glass petition and spooked an unfortunate man on the other side.

'Could you give me the name and phone number of a stable relative?' asked the woman in the polo neck quite calmly. 'Someone who has a settled lifestyle.'

I could hardly believe what she was saying. Had my behaviour been noticeably unusual? I ran a quick check through all the relatives. It was impossible to judge who was the most stable and worthy of being saddled with my debts. I gave out my mother's statistics, including her maiden name.

'Could I see something as proof of your signature?' she asked in her terribly tired voice.

By this stage I was totally numb and demoralised.

'If I pay this off before six months, I won't have to pay any extra money, right?' I asked.

'Yes, just sign here, please,' she said, pointing to the $49 interest I would have to cough up if I took a year to pay it off.

'That's certainly what I intend to do,' I said. 'Pay it off quickly, I mean.'

'Could you just initial that, please?' she said, interrupting my hesitant sentences.

She had heard it all before.

It looks as if consumerism is here to stay. Nowhere is it more poignant than in the toy supermarket. There's something sadly grotesque about those places. Toys should be about love. They ought to be made by little old men with grey hair and half-moon spectacles. They shouldn't be spat out by the trillion from machines full of plastic.

In an ideal world, toys would be given away in equal portions to all children. But, seeing love tokens must earn money like everything else, they could at least be sold from magic grottoes by people who know about life.

The idea of a supermarket full of toys to be raked off shelves, shoved into trollies and wheeled past check-out girls makes me feel unwell. It's as if people are terrified there isn't enough love in one or two small things any more. They want Christmas for their kids every day. Television tells kids they need Christmas every day.

I pulled into the carpark almost by mistake. The baby was fixated by her big brother's soccer ball, but no way would he share it with her. It had to be enshrined in his bedroom, touched by no one who was likely to subject it to indignities such as bouncing down the hall.

The soccer ball had been a love present. It had given joy, but had also created its share of problems. I figured they'd go away if the baby had her own ball to bounce around.

That's all I wanted, I reminded myself as I slung her on my hip and headed through the swing doors. A ball for the baby. I was struck by the same empty feeling I always get when I stroll down aisles of dolls, trucks, guns and Garfields. We were assailed by banks of plastic colour, forests of safety-sewn eyes and mountains of non-flammable fur.

The baby was overwhelmed by the spectacle for a moment or two. She cooed with wonder. But it didn't take long for her to cotton on that this was more than a television show. When she realised the toys could be touched and slobbered over, she squirmed to get down. I wished I'd brought the pushchair.

We fought our way through the corridors of affluence till we found the ball department. Choosing a baby's ball isn't as simple as it sounds, not in a toy supermarket. There are beach balls, basketballs, footballs, big ones with hearts and small multi-coloured ones. Most of them are made of plastic.

I know it's a wonderful material — cheap, colourful and versatile — but sometimes I wonder if kids get sick of the cool, smooth feel of it. There used to be many more textures when toys were made of wood, cloth and rubber.

A woman in a fake fur coat sorted through a nest of footballs with her child. Her mouth was a line. Her face joyless. The kid wasn't having fun, either. The child rolled a small red sphere along the concrete floor, but didn't bother chasing it.

'What *do* you want?' the mother yelled.

Her voice boomed across the supermarket, echoing the cries of parents the city over. The underlying question was: If I buy you this, will it make you happy? Will you love me a little more? Remember me when you're grown up with a warmer light in your eye?

She thrust a medium-sized football at him.

I always thought shares were something to do with sheep

'You can have it, but we're not made of money.'

As they carried their booty away, I lost enthusiasm. All the mothers in the toy supermarket wore the same haunted expression.

The baby made a beeline for a soccer ball just like her brother's. That would create more problems. I found one that looked like Jupiter. She seemed neither to like nor dislike it. I latched it under one arm, the baby under the other and headed for the checkout.

The baby wriggled herself to the ground to see the teddies. I want to give her everything — zoos full of bears — but in my heart I know she doesn't want everything. She needs that amorphous thing which is more difficult to define. Love.

The checkout girl put the ball in a brown paper bag and said, 'Have a nice day.' The air outside seemed remarkably fresh, clean and free. I tried to ignore the miserable mothers who were herding their offspring into cars. I strapped the baby into the car seat and gave her the ball to hold.

She wailed as we departed. I assumed she'd dropped the ball. I turned to see it wasn't the ball, but the paper bag it came in that she was crying for.

MORAL: She who visits toy supermarket shall leave with crying child.

9

Magic is for the nerds

AN ANTARCTIC blast hit my face when I opened the door. A streetlight caught the jagged rain outside. A small figure stood in the dark on the doorstep. He seemed strangely unaware of the storm — as if it was something he had created and carried around with him all the time.

His raincoat nearly touched the ground. He carried a suitcase so large he could have curled up inside it. There were two small wooden boxes in the other hand. An emerald green beret was pulled down to his eyebrows, giving him a bizarre appearance. But underneath, his eyes were serene and wise.

'It's the magician!' I called to the kids.

Unimpressed, as boys tend to be, they kept on playing pass-the-parcel. They hurled the newspaper bundle at each other, issuing taunts and accusations. I decided the magician was a terrible mistake. How could such world-wise dwarfs, drunk on television and movies, begin to appreciate something as simple as an old man doing tricks?

I felt sorry for him as he prepared his show in the kids' bedroom. The little beggars would slay him. They rolled restlessly on the living room floor when he appeared wearing a false nose, glasses, a fez, bowtie and sash. They hardly noticed him setting up two tables in front of the gas fire. I wanted to wring their necks.

In the sad, grating voice of a circus clown, he introduced his first trick: a picture of two birds sitting on a wall. He covered them with a scarf.

'Have the dicky birds gone?' He peered under scarf. 'Yes, they have.'

The audience jeered. I began to fear for his safety.

'And do you know why they've gone?'

He lifted the scarf to reveal a cat where the birds had been.

Magic is for the nerds

'You turned it round!' someone scoffed.

'Oh, did I?'

The magician turned the picture to show a wall free of cats or dicky birds. They had been fooled, but were too cool to show it. I led a round of applause.

A boy tweaked a balloon with irritating regularity. Another lolled back in an armchair. Was it a matter of time before they had him chained in the bath with the water running?

His hands were large and square, but every trick was performed without a fumble. He made ropes change their lengths in a plastic bag. Dirty scarves washed themselves clean in a cardboard box. Then there was the disappearing ping-pong ball.

'It's in your mouth!' they yelled.

'Ut ish nuf in m'muff,' he replied.

They jeered and demanded proof. I cringed for the man when he opened his mouth. Miraculously, it was empty. Carefully, modestly and with considerable expertise, he wove a spell across the room. When he announced the last trick, silence fell.

'What could I make with this sheet of white paper?' he asked.

'An origami frog,' our son said. 'You know, the ones you blow up the bottom?'

The magician looked genuinely horrified.

'I've heard of little boys doing that,' he said. 'How would you like it if I got a vacuum cleaner hose and . . . ? You mustn't do that to frogs. They're only human.'

The magician tore an exquisite bird shape from the paper. He then screwed it up and put it in a box. When he opened the box and pulled out a real live racing pigeon, the audience drew a single breath. They crowded around the bird and stroked its head. Wonder glowed on their faces — till they checked themselves.

'It's cruel to keep it in a box.'

'It's only a dummy.'

I watched the little man, magician no more, pack his tricks back into the case.

'It's better when you don't get so many interruptions,' he said.

Over a cup of tea and a chocolate crackle, he told me of the days he had performed in the town hall and on television. He'd been doing magic for 50 years. By day, he'd worked as a plumber, but it was obvious where his heart belonged. Now, at 74, he did old people, sports clubs, kindergartens and children's parties.

'There's four magicians working in town,' he said. 'Only two of them will do kids.'

The magician pulled down his beret, gathered up his suitcase and boxes and headed for the door.

'Say thank you,' I said to the kids, half-expecting them to scowl. Instead, they let out a roar of approval. The magician left the house with boyish bellows of gratitude echoing in his head. I hope that sound made it worth his while.

It's nice to know some old-fashioned things still have relevance today. Even something as ancient as *The Good Book.*

We have become potential burglary victims, at last. I don't know if I should feel pleased or sorry. The video machine doesn't look particularly desirable. I still can't work out how to use the timer to record programmes while I'm asleep.

But it's got to be great. It means our son can record the rubbish he watches after school and regurgitate it any time he likes. We, on the other hand, can capture the endless arty plays they televise late at night. By the time we've put the kids to bed and watched the news, however, we're too worn out to sit in front of a black and white 1940s classic.

While the tapes of worthy productions mount up in one corner of the living room, we keep the old exhausting routine — and remain as uneducated as ever. But I mustn't be too harsh. It's fair to say the video recorder has taught us more than any other appliance in the house. The thing it's taught us most about is fear.

Even before we bought it we were scared of being ripped off. We started in a seedy shop that reeked of cats. It had Amazingly Low Prices spray painted in radiant colours on the window.

The salesperson, who looked like a cast member of the *Rocky Horror Show,* tried to dazzle us with technology. He was definitely the type who sells it to you one day and nicks it the next.

In the end, we bought a video from a bland young man in a department store. As soon as we got the thing home, my husband wanted to wrap it in chains and solder it to the wall. I talked him out of it. He settled for welding our name on the side and smothering it with invisible ink.

I'm frightened of burglars, too. I don't want them smashing windows and tromping through the house. If they really want our video, I'd rather leave it in the letter box with the tapes of arty plays.

The damned machine has taught us another fear, as well. It has the potential to expose the kids to all sorts of sex and violence. The sex doesn't worry me if it's nice, cuddly stuff that involves mutual respect.

Violence is another matter. There's enough violence going on among the insects in the backyard without him watching car smashes, knives plunging into flesh and faces streaming with blood. When we visited the shop, I was horrified to see him head for the violence corner.

'How about *Walt Disney's Cartoon Parade*?'

'Kids' stuff!' he snarled.

We went home empty-handed. The prints on the living room wall shuddered as he slammed his bedroom door. I wondered if there were any part-time burglars I could ring up to take the video away. When he emerged, I prepared for video wars to recommence.

'Mum', he said softly, 'will you read to me from the *Bible?*'

'What?' My ears had gone on the blink. 'You mean the book about God and Jesus?'

He nodded. It had to be a trap. No kid asks for the *Bible*.

'We're doing a play about Joseph and his coat at school. It's a choice story.'

Somewhere near the dawn of parenthood, I'd bought a children's *Bible*. It's been used for pressing spiders, throwing at people and propping up chairs. But never for reading. In a haze of disbelief, I dug it out of a dark corner. The kid sat expectantly at my feet. We looked like an Edwardian lithograph.

' "Jacob loved Joseph more than all his sons, because he was the son of his old age, so he made for him a coat of many colours. . ." '

It wasn't long before the violence began. The brothers ripped off his coat and thought about murdering him. They threw him into a pit, then changed their minds and sold him to the Ishmaelites. As if that wasn't bad enough, they dipped the coat in blood and broke the old man's heart by telling him Joseph was dead.

As a matter of fact, Joseph isn't all that lovable himself. When he's thrown in gaol, he's kind enough to tell some bloke the Pharaoh is going to hang him on a tree and the birds will eat his flesh within three days.

When Joseph becomes a hot shot in Egypt, he's pretty rough on the peasants, too. Through seven years of famine, he makes them give their land to the Pharaoh in exchange for food. Hardly welfare state. Joseph and his brothers get back together — but not till after Joseph has given them a hard time.

'That's great,' he sighed when I finished. 'More tomorrow?'

I thumbed through the pictures of slave lashings, plagues of lice and Egyptians being drowned.

At least it's cheaper than the violence on hire at the video shop.

No matter how hard you try to economise on keeping kids happy, there's one time of year that's always going to cost you.

He wants an electronic digital radio alarm clock for Christmas. I know because he has asked a thousand times. He has also cut out a newspaper advertisement for the clock, pinned it to the kitchen wall and called it 'the most beautiful picture in the world'. It has a price tag of $38.95.

'But you have one already,' I said.

I'm particularly fond of it because my father brought it back as a present when he went overseas many years ago. The boy was privileged to receive it when we bought a more souped-up version for our bedroom.

'But it's not electronic and it hasn't got a radio.'

'But you have a radio already,' I said. 'In fact, you have three.'

'They haven't got alarm clocks.'

In an exasperated way, I began to see his point. But then I remembered my own childhood Christmases. The gifts that stand out most in my mind are a blue and white striped playsuit that Mum made. And a plastic blow-up doll that squeaked when you touched it. I never wanted to let the air out of that doll because it contained the breath of Father Christmas.

Unfortunately, it wasn't very well made. The great man's air soon seeped through the plastic seams and gave the doll a crumpled, disillusioned look. I don't mean to sound too materialistic about these things, but neither of those gifts would have cost more than ten dollars on today's market. Yet they're what I remember.

Kids these days are probably as bad as the adults. They value things not for what they are, but what they cost. When we visited the zoo the other day, I told him a true story that had beguiled me as a child. My older sister had always been timid. She was four when she met her first hippo. It opened its giant yawning mouth at her. She threw her handbag at it and ran away screaming.

He considered the story and said, 'How much was in the handbag?'

I suppose some would say $38.95 would be getting off lightly for a ten year old. But why couldn't he ask for something simple, meaningful and cheap? Like a fluffy bath cleaner.

Christmas is full of odd injustices. You rush around buying gifts for closest friends and family and cards for people you haven't seen in years. The average card sender would recognise only half the people on his or her Christmas card list if they appeared on the front doorstep.

In the meantime, there are hordes of perfectly nice people who have been generous and thoughtful throughout the year. They aren't close enough for presents, or remote enough for cards. So they are Christmas unrecognised.

'And I thought Father Christmas might like to give me a Garfield sweatshirt,' he said like an accountant at the end of the financial year.

Somewhere along the way, we had fallen into a terrible trap with Father Christmas. We must have been delirious with generosity the year we let them have a present from the jolly man as well as something from us, the parents.

'You don't still believe in Father Christmas?' I said, feeling the bank balance sink even further into the depths of overdraft. His mouth twisted wryly. I'd only recently read an American survey that said most kids are seven when they become non-believers. Thank God he wasn't backward.

'How long have you known?'

His expression was noncommittal. The survey said most kids were untraumatised by the discovery. The majority learned about the FC fraud from friends, while others matched handwriting and wrapping paper and worked it out for themselves.

'We found the presents under your bed years ago,' he said. 'You never were any good at hiding things.'

'Well, why didn't you tell us?'

I knew the answer would be deeply depressing. The child rubbed his nose on his sleeve and stared at the ceiling.

'We didn't want to hurt your feelings.'

10

Is there a name for women who sleep with midgets?

HOTELIERS CAN'T help it. They always get a cynical glint in their eye when you ask for a room for two.

'Double, is it?' she said, eyeing me like a magpie over her spectacles.

'Well, there are two of us.'

Her eye slid across to my tall, increasingly handsome, but ten-year-old son.

'So you want a double bed?'

'Oh no!' I said, blushing and taking an involuntary step backward. 'I mean this is my son.'

She didn't believe one syllable. Either I was a cradle snatcher, or I had a thing about midgets.

'We do have a twin suite, but it has private facilities,' she said as if this was bad news.

'How much is that?'

'Ninety-two dollars.'

It really was out of our league. A silence.

'There is a cheaper one with a double bed,' she said, staring sceptically through the sliding glass petition.

'I'm not sleeping with *her*!' the child bellowed across the foyer.

'Silly, isn't it?' I said to the magpie lady. 'I suppose most people you get ask for twins when they really want doubles, and here we are doing the opposite.'

One side of her mouth twitched. It was either the semblance of a smile or she'd had a sudden pain in her intestines.

'I'm sure we can manage something. Is it a very big double bed?' I asked.

Her eye remained expressionless, unblinking. You couldn't blame her. Hotel people see everything. Just the other day, one was telling me she had people turning up in the middle of the

Is there a name for women who sleep with midgets?

night with no luggage, demanding a bed. It was the lack of luggage that impressed me. Amazing to think there are people with so much style.

'I'll *die* if I have to sleep with you!' he yelled.

Frankly, I wasn't too keen on the prospect of his company, either. When the remnants of childhood send him bounding into my bed at home after the odd nightmare, it's been impossible. He's delivered enough karate chops to classify me as a mugging victim.

I tried to explain that the alternatives at this hour in a remote country town weren't dazzling. It would be a case of sleeping bolt upright in the car, or fighting it out with mosquitoes on a patch of damp grass.

'Have you got any barriers?' he asked the magpie woman.

For once, she seemed curious.

'You know, something to put down the middle of the bed.'

'Excuse me,' an assertive female voice piped up over my shoulder. 'Have you got a double room for the night?'

I turned to face two huge floral breasts. Above them towered an intimidating jaw and the face of a woman in her 50s who was obviously used to getting her own way. An invisible bolt of antagonism passed between us as we prepared to battle for the only double bed in the house.

'Look, I just work behind the bar,' the magpie woman said. 'I'll go get Mabel.'

Just when I was beginning to wonder if Mabel was an imaginary being, a small, hunched woman appeared behind the glass and said 'yesssss?' in the generous gap between her front teeth.

'We don't mind a double bed as long as it's a big one,' I said, loud and fast, all sense of shame gone.

'But you'd really like two singles?'

'As long as it's not too expensive.'

'Well,' she said, running a bony finger down the list of lucky names who had a place to lay their heads. 'You could try room six. No facilities. Forty dollars. Pop upstairs and have a look.'

Half-suspecting a trick, I bounded up the red and orange staircase to find the room surprisingly perfect. I knew he'd want the bed by the window.

'Hey! This is great!' he said. 'I can see two car lots and some brown sea.'

I adore staying in ageing hotels. The smells, the outrageous carpets, the breakfasts and the astonishing people who frequent them have me enthralled. However, I always land the room directly above the public bar. It was Saturday and the jukebox was already vibrating the floorboards.

'This will really rock me to sleep,' he said, grinning broadly at his own wit. 'Get it?'

Down in the elaborately decorated dining room, he had the grace to order from the children's menu. The woman in the floral dress had also been in luck. Her breasts rested gratefully on the tablecloth next to ours as she studied the menu.

Her man was like a semi-transparent shrimp. He was a small, grey person with all sense of individuality well crushed out of him.

'They've got Gainsborough's "Blue Boy" on the wall over there,' he said in an eerie contralto.

'Yes, I know dear,' she said, not moving her eye from the entree. 'But it won't be the real thing. It's probably just a copy.'

Now he's getting older, we are able to have fun together. Once I even decided to embark on a cycling mission with him.

Every now and then, a woman wants to do something for her son. Something he will remember for the rest of his life as symbolic of their relationship.

'You want to go cycling with him this weekend?' a friend said. 'Take my old ten-speed. I've hardly ridden it.'

The machine in her basement was elegant to look at.

'But how do you ride on a seat like that?' I asked.

'They're all that shape.'

'People aren't made that way, are they?'

'You'll get used to it.'

There were just a few pointers, she said. Don't use the front wheel brakes in an emergency. And don't use the back brakes one at a time or you'll go straight over the handlebars. She clambered on and wobbled up the road.

'Just keep pedalling when you want to change gear,' she shouted.

'How do I know when to do that?'

'You'll just have to work it out for yourself,' she said. 'Pull the seat up a bit. Oh, and never *never* pedal backwards.

Her tone was so grim, I didn't dare ask what would happen then. Our own road was too steep to practise on. Instead, I searched the town for something to make the seat softer.

'You mean you want a numbum,' the bike shop man said without a gleam of a smile.

'I beg your pardon?'

'It's the most popular in our range,' he said, producing a padded vinyl cover.

'Are you sure you can ride that thing?' my husband said as mother and son set off up the road.

'I will by the time we get back.'

They say ten-speeds are great for going up hills. But I couldn't find the right gear. I had to get off and push. The main road was busy with Saturday morning traffic. At least it was flat. I scrabbled on the thing to find myself in a humiliating position, crawling along the road with eyes set on the anorexic front wheel below me.

It was impossible to see more than one inch ahead. Let alone the scenery. A lamp-post suddenly reared up in front of me. Nobody had said how to steer the wretched thing. It seemed hellbent on confrontation. A split second before disaster, I hauled it sideways.

'You're doing great,' he called from the sanity of his BMX. 'You hardly puffed coming down that last hill.'

I whizzed past him like a blowfly.

'Hang on a minute! You've lost your . . . seat!'

He sped after me, seat-of-unmentionable-name flapping from one handlebar. It didn't seem to matter if it was on or off. I was in agony.

'How do people go any distance on these things?' I asked a man outside a country store.

'Oh you get hardened to them, if you know what I mean,' he said. 'I knew someone who cycled round the world. But she had to have an operation halfway through.'

'Ah! Smell that!' the boy said when we'd pushed our bikes to the top of another hill. 'Fresh air!'

Freesias nodded in the grass. A rooster crowed in the distance. The smile on his face made the pain go away. For a moment. I prepared for descent.

'Don't start on the gravel,' he said. 'Or you'll . . .'

I was beginning to tire of his continuous encouragement and instruction.

'. . . fall off. See? I told you.'

Ten-speeds prefer smooth, civilised concrete. Let loose on

rugged country roads, they become self-destruct kits on wheels. Once I'd mustered pride and started again, it was a matter of trying to dodge the bigger stones. When I stood on the pedals to avoid seat contact, the balance changed and I remembered the straight-over-the-handlebars routine.

'Of course, ten-speeds are easier if you've been riding an ordinary bike lately,' said the man on the road. 'But if you haven't ridden since you went to school you're bound to find it . . . hard.'

So that's what it was. When things got bad, my companion reminded me how much better, faster and further Dad would have been. I reminded him that Dad had been offered my place with heartfelt sincerity, and declined.

Sometimes, I ignored the pain and almost enjoyed the mixture of terror and excitement involved in hurtling down hills. After a steep one, I decided to make a go of getting up the next one on wheels. I kept pedalling and fiddled with the gears only to hear a nasty crunching sound. The pedals had jammed.

'Do you know anything about ten-speeds?' I asked a woman in a garden shop.

'No, but Bob should.'

An amiable fellow with red skin and blond eyelashes attacked the back wheel with a spanner.

'You've lost your chain here, see? You've been pedalling backwards, haven't you?' he said, waving his spanner at me. 'You must never *never* . . .'

'I know. Could you tell me which gears are which?' I asked.

He rubbed his hands on a grubby handkerchief and said he didn't know much about ten-speeds. Soon after, I tried to introduce the kid to the joys of walking. Except in my case it was a saddle-sore swagger. Maybe John Wayne had a ten-speed, too.

As the day wore on, the task of finding a bed for the night loomed ahead. The guesthouse man turned us away. I chose to believe him when he said he didn't have room left. But I couldn't help noticing an empty unit with spotlessly made-up twin beds.

A bedraggled mother and son clutching their bikes probably didn't look like his sort of clients. He sent us down a winding dirt road to a youth hostel. Budget accommodation, he said, looking at the tear in my trousers.

I wasn't comfortable about the idea of a youth hostel. It was bound to be full of spotty young things playing space invaders. What if they had an age limit? I could try arguing that together our average age was twenty and a half.

The setting was enchanting. A crimson peaked roof rose gracefully out of the bush. We bumped our bikes over tree roots and knocked on the door. An upstairs window opened and a face appeared. A pair of intense brown eyes peered out through two curtains of hair that hung down either side of his face.

'Have you got any room?' I called.

'Hang on a minute.'

When he reappeared at ground level, I was relieved to see he had crow's-feet. He wore thongs over a pair of thick woollen socks. Harry was the name. He didn't notice the rip in my trousers.

'I like to keep the cabins for couples,' he said. 'They need a bit of privacy. You can have one if a couple doesn't turn up. In the meantime, I'll put you in the dormitory.'

The word reeked of miserable childhoods of biscuit tins under beds, and torches that shine unbidden into eyes in the depths of night. We paused at the SHOES OFF! sign and padded over rush matting upstairs to a vast sleeping room. I expected my son to rebel when he saw his humble mattress on the floor inside a curtained-off compartment. He belongs to the electric blanket, duvet generation. He took it calmly.

Harry gave us sheets and grey blankets and assured us the pillowcases were clean. As I tested my mattress (which wasn't too bad) I tried to imagine what the room would be like at midnight, full of adolescent ravers. The paintings of Hieronymus Bosch would have nothing on this.

Down in the commonroom, a woman with red hair brooded into her glass of mineral water. She was no spring chicken, either. Pale and thin, she was prone to long silences and endless walks alone. I decided she was recovering from a breakdown of some sort.

When she muttered something about not liking children, my kid blurted loud sexual jokes to prove he was a man trapped in unfortunate wrapping.

Out in the kitchen, where you must identify your milk and leave no stale food, I met another elderly youth.

'I can't sleep,' he said. 'My girlfriend left me three days ago. My body's all hyped up and my head goes round and round all night.'

'You'll go through it again one day if you're lucky,' I said. 'It's only love.'

'But it's *terrible*!'

Harry seemed to have his own troubles. He slept all day. At night, he knocked back large slugs of neat whisky and became a warm and loving host. He dragged out old magazines for three not-so-cheerful divorcees to look at, and played ruthless chess with my son.

As I tucked the offspring into his compartment around 9 p.m., a nearby curtain let out a terrible moan. It was Romeo trying to sleep.

'Aren't you taking a cabin?' he said. 'I moved out so you could have it.'

'No, you keep it,' I insisted.

He gathered up his blankets and stumbled off into the night. Back downstairs, Harry roped the divorcees, a handsome American and me into a gambling card game called Swim. It was simpler than poker, so I could begin to understand it. We invested a dollar each.

The American, who had a German girlfriend who was too shy to emerge from their cabin, delivered a speech on the general wunnerfulness of the American people. In turn, Harry praised his own country to the sky.

At midnight, I realised with some embarrassment I'd won. I stuffed six dollars worth of coins into my pocket and said I'd buy something for the common good with it in the morning.

'None of that communist rubbish,' one of the divorcees said. 'You keep it.'

Next morning, I bought a large fruit loaf with raspberry icing on top, and handed it around. Although the fading youths disapproved in theory, they fairly wolfed it down.

11
Pacific Island shells

I PICKED it up for ten dollars in a tourist shop. It was a flamboyant necklace made of yellow coral interspersed with three wooden bananas. The men in our group were busy buying stuff to take home to their wives. They sifted coyly through the dress racks and deemed most of the Polynesian styles too extrovert.

I'd never realised men put so much thought into the traveller's presents they nudge so offhandedly across the kitchen table back home.

'It's not devotion, it's fear,' one said, holding a pair of dainty earrings up to the light.

Another stretched a T-shirt with coconut fronds printed on the front across his chest.

'We're not the same size,' he said with a faint blush. 'She suits blue.'

None of them went for the necklace with the bananas. Maybe they all had wives with conservative taste — or was that how they perceived their women? Either way, I felt guilty buying something for myself when everyone else was being so unselfish. But I couldn't resist the necklace.

I meant to keep it to wear in the grey winter back home. But the necklace begged to be worn in the expansive summer of the Cook Islands. I put it on for the first time when we visited the tiny island of Mitiaro.

It's one of those places that makes you feel pity and envy at the same time. The people live off the land and sea. If they get extra fish in their catch, or more produce than they need, they send it to friends and relatives, free of charge, on other islands. They haven't learnt to worship money yet.

As a result, they are what we call poor. They don't have televisions and hospitals and carpets. Every now and then, someone on Mitiaro begins to think they're missing out. They fly to bigger countries to get jobs. Their intention is clear. They'll save money and return to Mitiaro to build a home.

It never seems to work out that way, however. They learn a lot of things in the richer countries. They learn about violence and crime that's virtually unheard of on their own island. More than anything, they learn how to put money ahead of the land and sea.

When they return to their island, they find it hard to understand why their relatives are happy at subsistence level. And the relatives certainly don't understand them.

Yes, the people of Mitiaro are poor. But they are also very rich. They have the spirituality that materialistic Westerners now crave. The people of Mitiaro are so wealthy they can still smile — not because they want something, or someone has done something stupid, or they feel insecure. They smile with the sheer joy of being alive. It takes a while to get used to that kind of affluence.

'I like it here,' one woman sighed with deep contentment. 'It's quiet.'

She'd learned to teach on Rarotonga for a while. But the shops and hotels and roads were too noisy. On Mitiaro she can raise her children and become part of the land and sea and sky.

The woman spoke of her four-week-old baby. It hadn't been easy. They'd flown her to Rarotonga for a difficult birth.

'I like your necklace,' she said, tactfully changing the subject.

I began to recall someone had once said that in this part of the world it's polite to make a gift of any focus of admiration. To be honest, I felt threatened. I'd grown specially fond of the necklace, and knew there wouldn't be another like it.

'Oh, really?' I said. 'Thank you.'

'Where did it come from?'

Another island, 30-odd miles away. But to her, the distance was vast. If she ever got there with ten dollars in her hand, there's no way she'd spend it on a banana necklace. The thing was as unique to her as it was to me.

'You have it,' I said, beginning to feel warm inside.

She seemed genuinely taken aback. Maybe it wasn't this part of the world that had the custom, after all. I'd made up my mind, anyway. It was logical she should have it.

'For your baby,' I said, unhitching it from my neck and handing it over.

Her face beamed like the noon sun and she disappeared into a forest of coconut trees. The wind rustled in the fronds and I thought she wasn't coming back. Ten minutes later, she turned up clutching her baby in a white blanket. Around its sleeping neck she'd latched the banana necklace. The ornament seemed vast against such a tiny human. It nearly reached the baby's feet.

In her other hand, she held a small bottle of beer. An unusual, but touching gift, I thought. She explained it was full of oil. I prised the lid open and sniffed a heady combination of coconut oil and beer.

'For sunburn or anything,' she said mysteriously.

When we said goodbye, it felt as if we had known each other a long time. The rest of the group seemed amused when I told them the story. That night at dinner, one of them, who had a Pacific Island heritage himself, presented me with a similar necklace made of red coral and strawberries.

Back home, a beer bottle sits on my kitchen window ledge. During cold months the oil sets hard and white. It's been used to rub the winter ache from my son's neck and to soften a patch behind the baby's ear. The effect is almost magical.

In summer, the oil melts and makes an unusual tan lotion with a perfume that usually prompts remarks.

I like to keep the strawberry necklace at hand, too. Both it and the coconut oil are precious beyond words.

The gently loving atmosphere of Mitiaro was a strong contrast to what our visit to the Cooks was all about. We were there to make war games, not love.

A planeload of potatoes, wimps, a girl and a few real men takes off from the militiary base. If there's anyone to blame for the delay, it's the potatoes. Several hours were spent shuffling their bulk around to balance the plane. It's unwise to begrudge them the VIP treatment. They are, after all, very important potatoes. If all goes well, they'll soon be filling the stomachs of hungry service men and women in Rarotonga.

The thirteen journalists don't look very trustworthy with their earnest faces and arty paperbacks. They're definitely wimps. The fact there's a girl among them isn't a good sign.

The Boeing has no carpet on the floor. But you don't expect luxury on your way to war. It was built in 1965 — around the time a lot of the uniformed passengers were born.

As the plane grinds over the Pacific, some of the journalists cry out for alcohol. But this is war. Booze is allowed only if a VIP is on board. A bigwig is sprawled on the front seats, but he's only a Fairly Important Person. It's water laced with lime, or nothing.

Rarotonga night enfolds us like a hot, wet towel as we head toward the immigration officials.

'First time I've arrived on a Pacific Island without being instantly lei-ed,' says the man from Reuters. Laughter is obligatory.

The army marches us to its camp. Flapping tents and the smell of crushed grass are reminiscent of a fairground. But the party's over when we're shuffled into a tent for the first of many briefings.

A slightly nervous officer tells us what we should know. There are nine thousand people on Rarotonga, another nine thousand on outer islands. They're shy but friendly, God-fearing people. It's important not to badmouth anyone because it's liable to get back. He hints that some chiefs on outer islands are keen not to have their young women interfered with.

As he steps back, a regimental sergeant major moves forward. He's built like a bull. Purple veins stand out on his neck. His teeth jut out like little white bullets. He clears his throat and lets out a series of barks.

'My name is sir!' he says. 'To me fornication means another word, and I won't say it because there are ladies present! We are here to work! If you think you're here for a holiday, you can get back on the plane and go home!'

He glances at the cringing journalists and reassures them the information is mainly for the troops.

'No thongs in town and no rough stuff like "The Air Force Sucks" on your T-shirts!'

With his crewcut and tiny fierce eyes, he could have walked straight out of a B-grade war movie. There seems something almost schizophrenic in his attitude. The whole world is divided into sirs and lads. He talks to sirs in a gentle nanny's voice as he directs them to their tents. Lads, on the other hand, get treated as if they've just murdered their mother.

'Six to a tent, lads!'

Only the mention of ablutions changes his mood.

'I smile because some of you journalists won't be used to them,' he says in a sinister tone.

Half-broken already, we shuffle to our sleeping quarters.

'Keep to the path,' a voice advises after I've fallen in the mud twice.

'How can we sleep with those frogs in the grass?' one of the journalists says.

'You mean there are frogs as well?'

'What else is making that noise?'

'That's crickets. Somerset Maugham, remember?'

One of the journalists refuses to enter his tent till the light is on. I share an abode with two women who have such an active social life they're seldom home. Pillows, they say, will arrive tomorrow. They never do.

Over in the mess, we sit on planks hoping food will materialise.

'There's no dinner,' says a young man who has frank blue eyes, 'because if we'd been on time, the meal on the plane would have been lunch. Except we weren't so it was dinner.'

It takes a while to get used to military logic.

Some locals have set up a piecart on the way to the ablutions. It sells blue icecreams, postcards, condoms and thirty-five-dollar bottles of not very classy-looking perfume. I settle for a hot dog. The moon sits like a boat in the sky. Stars stand out like crystals you could reach out and touch. There haven't been so many, so clear, since I was a child.

'Here, have a Mintie,' says a voice.

He thrusts a sticky lolly into my hand. All this and Minties too.

A bed made of pineapple leaves would be only slightly less comfortable than the stretcher. The bald light globe glares in my eyes. Someone whistles 'Rule Britannia' outside.

After midnight, a male conversation starts up across the path.

'She's nice, eh? Really nice. She gave me her number, but I can't remember her name.'

My tentmates bowl in around 2 a.m. and are horrified to find another occupant. I pretend to sleep as they fumble with my suitcase to read the name on the label.

'I can't sleep with that bloody thing on.'

Straining noises and more giggles as they move a large object around. I open one eye a crack to see a semi-naked woman standing on a trestle to remove the lightglobe. She loses balance, shrieks, sails through the air and lands on top of me.

Next morning, they tell me about their jobs. One is an air force mechanic. The other is in stores. When they learn what I do, they lock up their valuables and try not to answer any questions, not even about the time. The military is so deeply suspicious of the media that I begin to wonder if we've been brought here for target practice.

That night, I try to improve relations by accepting an invitation to drink and dance with junior officers in town. In many ways, they represent manhood in its prime. Bodies developed to perfection, well groomed and supremely confident. Those who served in Vietnam speak of death and pain with no fear. Their eyes cloud with uncertainty, however, when they talk of leaving the army. It's a young man's job on the whole. Those who aren't promoted quickly retire early.

One of them, in his late 30s, has handed in his notice. He wants to retrain in computers or marketing.

'I've got a lot of skills to offer,' he says, the lack of confidence showing in his voice.

Another wants to retire to a tiny village in East Yorkshire. He'll take his stereo gear and do manual labour.

The army is more than a marriage. It provides nourishment, accommodation and the knowledge you're okay as long as you do what you're told. The army is mother, father, gym instructor, doctor, wife and boss. Strip it away from some of these guys and it's easy to imagine they could, at best, take a while to adjust to civilian life.

The men who have seen the death and destruction of Vietnam seem set apart from the others. It's not just the fact they're older. Their toughness seems to have sunk several layers into their skin. They have seen the other side of sanity — hysteria, cruelty and murder. Yet they've decided to stick with the army. I suspect every one short of an automaton cracked up at some stage during the war.

'I tend to get into trouble when I say this,' one tells me, 'but I do enjoy war. It's what we're trained for.'

Even the tough guys aren't as tough as they seem. Unable to bear the multi-seated, sack-surrounded latrines at camp, they'd found a flush loo at the nearby airport terminal.

'It's not the lack of privacy that gets me,' says a Vietnam veteran. 'It's the smell and the look of them.'

Many camps exist within the cluster of olive green tents. Officers keep a distance from their men. The army finds the air force alarmingly disorganised and they seem to regard the navy as effeminate. The navy and air force think the army lacks intellect. None of the forces is enamoured of the media — and we're all self-conscious about the locals.

'Do the people of Rarotonga really like us?' someone asks as another Skyhawk booms overhead.

Most of them haven't seen soldiers before. Young local women are entranced by the uniforms and good looks. Small boys turn branches into guns and shoot each other dead.

We're loaded onto a Hercules headed for the island of Aitutaki. The journalists start like nervous owls at every unusual sound on this crazy form of transport. The army guys pretend to sleep so no one can witness their anxiety.

Aitutaki is a postcard come true. White sand stretches out to a sapphire sea. Tourists swim among the coral and sip coconut milk. A pair of them, drunk on romance, decide to get married on a sandbar.

Local drums rattle as the couple drift back to their hotel in a canoe. They kiss so often some people feel uncomfortable. Someone says they're Swedish. Met in Singapore, engaged in Hong Kong, married on Aitutaki and divorced in LA.

But it's war we're here for. There's something compelling yet disturbing about the mix of flags, soldiers and a Pacific haven of sensuality. The harshness of military things seems too much so, the lushness of the island too vulnerable.

Next morning, we're back at the airstrip watching the sun rise over the sea. The entire island got up before dawn to see something they'll never forget. The same officer who gave us our first briefing says we are to imagine the island has been overrun by enemy troops during the past week. A crack regiment has already arrived and weakened opposition on land.

We're about to see the good guys' final assault and victory. He says to expect a lot of loud bangs and stresses it's only pretend. A Skyhawk rises like a silver rocket in front of the sun. It glistens and looks extraordinarily beautiful. In a split second, it flicks and becomes menacing — a great black seagull of death swooping toward us.

The sound is deafening. It seems to be ripping the sky apart. The machine sweeps over the crowd and vanishes. It's well out of our sight when the ground shudders with explosions.

I feel a gush of fear, sorrow and pain for humanity. Tears well in my eyes. The horror of wars that have been surges through me. The knowledge that man goes on killing his own kind claws at my chest.

Just minutes ago, this had been paradise. Now it's a nightmare — death dressed up in expensive machinery for a rehearsal that's turned into a party. The crowd cheers for more. Skyhawks attack again and again.

The men are smiling. Their war comic fantasies have come true. But some women's jaws are set grimly. When you've hauled a small baby from your own body, your perception changes. There's a link among women who have produced children. No matter what their nationality, they understand the pain, the rewards of bearing children. They know what it is to love a child more than anything, including themselves.

To see a demonstration by an industry designed to demolish any mother's child is to be appalled to the core.

'Enjoying yourself?' one of the Vietnam veterans asks as he strides past.

He turns, sees my distorted face, and there's a flash of recognition in his eyes. Maybe he felt the same way on a real battlefield somewhere far from home. He offers neither comfort nor ridicule, but turns on his heel and walks away.

My legs take me through the crowd across to the beach. The sounds and smells of death still hover in the air as I pick over the coral and shells. The sea has washed them white as the dove of peace. I collect some to take home to my son.

12
People soup

WORK PEOPLE pretend not to see them as they hurry past on the way to their offices. But they're there almost every morning, sprawled, sometimes huddled, on the graffiti-scratched benches by the bus station.

They're not a lovely sight. Their bristly faces are flushed with too much booze. Their stained and ragged clothes would smell if you got too close. I try to ignore them, too, because I'm one of the harassed, panic-struck throng who whirl by. Old men in grubby coats and jerseys can be unpredictable, possibly even dangerous. They're used to getting the cold shoulder. They probably prefer it that way. But I can't help being interested.

There are usually two or three of them. It's difficult to tell if the same ones are there every day. Sometimes, the youngish-looking one with hair that's like greasy rope is replaced by an emaciated Father Christmas who dozes over his brown paper bag. The dark-skinned man with hurt brown eyes turns into one with ginger hair mown down to a few prickles and a graveyard cough.

Either way, there never seem to be enough teeth to go around. There's an air of understanding between them, as if they share the same view of the world. I sometimes wonder how they got that way. Were their domestic situations so disastrous that homeless outdoor living is preferable? Or was it simply the booze? Maybe the craving is so consuming nothing else matters. Were their fathers like that, too? If so, what happened to their mothers?

Under the grime, some of them have faces that would have been handsome once. Do they have wives somewhere in the suburbs, rearranging the net curtains before they settle down for a night's television?

If the women of their pasts ever do think of them, it's no doubt with a sigh of relief. Thank God I got rid of that bastard.

Work people know who are the winners and losers. That's why we ignore the tramps. But there's something unsettling about the men on the seat. They look at us as if we're the losers.

Perhaps they're really poets, the only ones with true perception of this selfish, materialistic world. Their awful clothes could be a protest. The scorn in their bleary eyes justifiable. When they spit on the pavement, maybe we should watch closely in case it's a statement.

They've usually gone by the time I leave work. The pubs are open and there's nothing for them to hang around for. But this afternoon was different. The rain started when I was standing at the intersection waiting for the lights. At first, it was like gentle dust leaving cobwebs on people's hair.

Then the air became swollen and heavy, as if something ripe was about to burst. The city greys grew darker as the clouds leaned down on us. As I stepped out on the road, a large drop of rain fell on my jacket. Dammit. I'd left my yellow raincoat hanging cool and dry in the laundry porch that morning.

None of the work people had brought their raincoats that day. Rain had not been on the weather forecast or on the memo from the boss. They hated getting wet, so they ran like startled ants.

I started running, too. It seemed to be expected. Trouble was there wasn't anywhere to run to. In that part of town the shops are low grade. Best bargain joints that don't have awnings.

A few people huddled together to shelter with smug looks on their faces in entrance ways. I was wet through already. There was no point fighting for a place. I slowed the run to a brisk walk and actually started to enjoy the drenching. As the rain flattened my hair against my face and sent drips falling from my chin, it seemed to rinse all my worries away.

When I strode around the corner by the bus station, I almost collided with one of the bench men. With arms waving like branches in a storm, old Father Christmas was engrossed in an unsteady dance.

Our eyes met for the first time. Two pagans revelling in a primitive rain festival. Then I remembered who he was, averted my eyes and trudged forward.

An office worker headed toward us. White shirt, walk shorts and a face wrinkled with anxiety. He had no idea how ridiculous he looked cringing under the briefcase on his head.

People soup

'Let the rain come down,' said Father Christmas to the worker under his briefcase. The voice was textured like wood shavings.

But the worker didn't understand. He hid further under his briefcase, and ran faster. Old Father Christmas sprung around and laughed up at the sky.

'Let the RAIN come down!' he bellowed.

He must have seen me smiling. He staggered along behind me and said in a suddenly quiet, cultivated voice: 'Have a good day.'

'You too,' I replied.

'I'll try,' he said, and shambled off into the soggy cityscape.

Not everyone you encounter in public places is pleasant. Sometimes the most respectable-looking people demonstrate the most depressing attitudes.

The first time I saw her on the bus I hardly noticed her. She was just another early morning face fresh out of the shower. As days passed, however, she became a familiar figure, always getting on and off at the same stops.

She's not the sort of person I warm to instantly. There's a crispness about her that suggests she has very definite ideas about right and wrong. Her mouth sits primly over a pointed chin. Her eyes are small and bright — quick rather than intelligent.

Yet I don't mean to be hard on her. She's had problems like everyone else. The lines on her face record some battles that she hasn't allowed to destroy her. She's come to terms with them. You have to respect someone for that.

A behavioural scientist would have a great time on a bus, studying what motivates people to choose certain seats. I have my own theory. The radicals sit at the back, adventurers go for seats over the wheels, conservatives sit somewhere near the middle and insecure people go near the front. The late ones take what they can get.

For some reason, this woman always sits close to me near the front. It's hard to imagine why she should feel comfortable in my company. Perhaps I remind her of a relative — or maybe she sees aspects of my personality that don't even exist.

I get a sinking feeling every morning as her brown pleated skirt marches down the aisle. She plonks her large vinyl shopping bag on the floor, stares into my face and wills me to start a conversation about the weather or the price of Fisher-Price toys. I studiously avoid her eye.

Some people say it's possible to send telepathic messages. If you say 'don't sit next to me' over and over in your head, the person will sense the negative vibrations and turn away. My transmitter seems to be faulty.

I tried sitting in a different part of the bus. It didn't work. She'd made up her mind that we were part of each other's morning and we belonged together. Nothing was going to deter a strong-minded woman like her.

No doubt her home life was equally well organised. A couple of nicely behaved kids on the verge of leaving home, an obedient husband who always remembered anniversaries. He had probably given her the tasteful gold chain around her neck this year.

She's a tidy person who half-believes the television advertisements and keeps a clean fridge.

One morning, I sat determinedly near the back, daring her to venture into radical territory. Calmly but surely, her Hush Puppies picked a path past the exit doors to the seat opposite mine. I stared glumly out the window.

At the next stop a young Polynesian woman headed toward us. She was exquisitely dressed in a pink tailored suit and her hair was meticulously plaited. The young woman turned gracefully, stirring the air with the exotic perfume of coconut oil, and sat just a little too close for comfort. In fact, I had to move sideways to separate our thighs.

That sort of thing doesn't bother me. I've landed too close to people often enough. But as I nestled against the window, I glanced at the woman opposite. There was a superior sparkle in her eye that implied women like us could afford to be amused. Her mouth was twisted in a smile that said 'What do you expect of people like that?'

She was revealing a horrific sisterhood I wanted no part of. When the woman in pink got off the bus, I wanted to go with her. But I had to stay on for another two stops.

On the occasions races mix more happily, everyone stands a lot to gain. Sometimes, even something as simple as a visit to a restaurant is like a brief but happy holiday abroad.

There's an air of expectancy about the waiters. They hover by the door and seem to almost sigh with relief when more customers arrive.

People soup

The couples who turn up with cheeks still flushed from the cold outside are pounced upon. Women are stripped of their coats and eagerly shown to tables. Their male partners, colonials to the core, lag sheepishly behind.

This isn't an ordinary restaurant, and these aren't usual waiters. Their highly developed sense of drama turns every event into a spectacle. Even finding a table becomes a soap opera. Would we like one close to the band, or perhaps an intimate corner? We choose the one jammed ominously close to a loudspeaker. He lights a small white candle on our table with a flourish.

It's not greed or fear of losing their jobs that motivates these dark-haired men with eyes on fire. It's simply the passion of dance.

Women complain about Greece. They say it's a terrible country to travel alone in. All Greek men assume fair-haired women have the morals of she-cats.

'It was terrible,' the seasoned traveller will say. 'I only wanted to buy a postcard and he followed me for two days. Two *whole* days! I didn't get a moment's peace.'

The same outraged female will fail to admit she had her hair bleached and her hems raised several notches just for the holiday. You can hardly blame the locals for getting confused, specially on the island of Lesbos which has become a Mecca for women of a certain persuasion.

The conservative Orthodox women in their long black gowns must wonder what they've struck when they see Joan and Dorothy locked in searing embrace on the street corner.

Having had a thoroughly exciting time themselves, women will tell you the only safe way to see Greece is with a man. (It's rather like the feminist prophets who had an amazingly promiscuous phase in the 1970s and now preach celibacy for everyone.)

Greek males will assume he's your husband, brother or father, who will cheerfully lay down his life for your innocence. Your lack of adventurous encounters will be assured.

'The music will start at 8.30,' says the waiter breathing heavily over my menu.

At about 8.20 the door bursts open and a small man strides into the room carrying a music case. His face, which is glowing, is an exact replica of a Greek doll's. When he sits on a high stool at the microphone, his eyes become hooded, he grows six feet tall and becomes irresistibly handsome.

The other two band members know their place. They're merely the sky on which the star will twinkle. They smile and make surreptitious eye contact with women customers, but quickly lower their eyes before any male patrons catch on.

The music is simple, vital and alive like sunshine. If you forget 'Zorba the Greek', 'The Lotus Eaters', 'Never On Sunday', and all the other tunes that made you hate Greek music, it's possible to learn to love it. How easy it must be for an emigrant to weep tears for his homeland to such strains.

At last, their moment has arrived. Two waiters link arms and plait their legs in delicate patterns — first slowly, then faster. An ageing American woman (hair still blond from her girlhood trip to Greece) lurches over, and hooks her arm across their shoulders.

They stagger slightly under her weight, but patiently adjust to her less practised steps and the occasional 'Whoopee!'

A tubby young local woman falls prey to their song and joins the chain. Two others throw off their shoes and make it longer. It takes more than an hour for any jokers to join in. Maybe they don't like being outshone by the waiters, whose jaws are now jutting with dignity.

By the time the local boys hit the floor they're blotto. They can't do any of the steps and instinctively try to scrum.

An elderly woman in black stands at the kitchen door. Her breasts are heavy and she's no longer beautiful. But it's as if everyone knows the next dance will be hers. She leads the American woman and two others onto the floor. Once more she's young, springing lightly over the boards, waving a tea towel in her free hand. There's an exuberance and pride in her dance, which seems to say much about relationships between women. When it's over, she's old again. She puts on a black coat and goes home.

Our own waiter beckons me to join him on the floor. It's pointless to resist. Greek dancing is more than running sideways, but it seems to get easier the faster you go.

A local joker grabs me by the neck instead of the shoulder and I wonder if there will be a front page strangulation in the paper tomorrow. Local Choker Strikes Again.

Toward midnight, the band plays some Beatles songs. The waiters rock 'n' roll while the local jokers start Greek dancing. We're among the last to leave.

13
Licensed to kill

NO MATTER how hard I try to be independent, assertive and modern, one thing still reduces me to pitiful whinings, crimson flushes and tears. When I got it a year ago, I thought it was clever to buy a mechanic's own car. He had cared for it as if it was a child. The alterations he had made to the old Volkswagen were the nurturing, corrective measures a father might make to improve his own son.

It felt like abduction the day I gave him the cheque and drove the car out of his driveway. I promised to bring it back for visits often. Trouble is it still feels like a stolen vehicle. The owner sits invisibly on my shoulder and grumbles at my driving faults and near-misses when I park it in the city.

If anything does go wrong (and this is not a young vehicle), I dread having to ring the mechanic to confess.

'Yes?' he says sharply. It's as if he senses I'm about to admit a sin.

'It's making a sort of vrooming noise.'

'Where?'

'In the engine. I think it's to do with the timing.'

'How often?'

'Well, all the time, I think. Specially at traffic lights.'

He gets irritated. And he has every right. Cars are probably simple things. It's pathetic that I'm reduced to ignorant burblings and baby talk. I curse the girls' school education that assumed we would all have husbands who would oil and grease the appropriate parts every weekend.

You didn't even have to know how to fill a petrol tank in those days. A nice man at the station would do it. At the bat of an eyelash, he would also pump up your tyres, check your oil and clean your windscreen.

Clouds of happiness

If your car broke down on the open road, battalions of eager gentlemen would rush to your rescue. Men felt protective towards anything in a skirt. We had hardly heard of assault and rape.

While we were busily learning to cook pikelets and sew gingham aprons, the boys across the valley were taught about cars, light fuses and how refrigerators work. I wish I'd been able to sit in on some of those lessons.

But we were all, to use an overly fashionable word, victims. It hadn't occurred to the education system that some of the girls might turn out as lesbian separatists and some of the boys as solo dads. The authorities worked on the basis that all men would have someone to make homes for them and all women would have a man to look after their mechanical gadgets.

The mechanic thinks I damage his car on purpose. He believes I have a mission to systematically destroy his motor and what little happiness there is left in his life.

'Oh, and by the way,' I say when he has fixed the automatic choke which has nothing to do with timing. 'There's also a sort of grating noise when I change gear.'

'A what?' he says, slitting his eyes.

'Well, it doesn't bother me too much as long as it's not causing any harm.'

'You need a new pressure plate,' he grunts.

'Just a minute. I'll write that down,' I say, trying to seem sincere in my efforts to be better educated.

'I'll have to take the engine out.'

It sounds horrifically expensive. He must feel a molecule of pity because he says it will only take an hour or so and it's not a great deal of trouble. Not if I drive across town, collect the parts and bring them back to him.

'I'm the woman with the clunkety Volkswagen,' I say to the spare parts man, who isn't impressed, either.

He's not sure what size pressure plate it will need, so he gives me two boxes (each with eighty dollar price tags) and asks me to bring back the one that doesn't fit.

As the car and I scrape and clunk back home, I worry. What if the engine falls out on the road? What's the point in driving around with two clutch plates in boxes and another that doesn't work in a car that doesn't even belong to you?

Tears well in my eyes. They're the stupid tears of a '50s dumb blonde who expects men to solve all her problems. I swear I'll go to night classes. I'll buy some overalls and learn to talk about overhead cams. Or start taking taxis.

Although cars are an essential part of the way we live, we often overlook the potential danger they involve. I don't often feel like hitting someone and trying to shake some sense into them.

The car wound down an attractive, leafy road. I could easily have been going faster, but it was a pleasant afternoon that had no hurry in it. There was plenty of time to enjoy the sun gleaming on green leaves. I lowered the side window to make the most of the fresh breeze on my face.

There was a pleasant rhythm in the way the car swung around the gentle bends to the bottom of the hill. When I turned the last corner, I wasn't prepared for the child. In fact, he was more a baby — no older than sixteen months.

He was the last thing I'd expected to see, standing nappy-clad on the kerb with his foot poised over the gutter. He was about to step out onto the road. If he'd moved fifteen seconds sooner, there would have been no way I could have stopped in time.

I spun past him, still trying to assemble my thoughts and imagine what insanity had resulted in a baby going to play on a road. There should have been a mother running white-faced and shocked to grab him to safety. But all I could see were two other pre-schoolers on tricycles.

I stamped on the brake, got out and ran back to the baby, who was now standing in the gutter and gazing thoughtfully over the street. His brothers had pedalled on down the road.

The small, mousy-haired child seemed unaffected by the panic-struck woman who swept him into her arms. Even through my jacket I could feel his disposable napkins were sodden, soiled and as cold as ice.

'Where's your mother?' I called to the mildly curious tricyclists.

'Long way.'

'You'd better show me.'

An unlikely foursome, we trudged up the hill past several letterboxes. The baby's flesh felt smooth and vulnerable in my hands. What chance would he have against a vast metal car?

The house was up a long, gravel driveway. It must have taken some time for the kids to have wandered so far. The house seemed deserted. Perhaps the mother was ill or, worse, had suffered some sort of domestic accident?

It was a modest place to put it politely. There were no carpets on the floor or pictures on the wall. Furniture was sparse. The front door was open. We stood outside in the eerie silence.

It was finally broken by the sound of a woman's voice, preoccupied. I made out her shape, thin and straw-haired, down the hall.

'Oh yes . . .' she said into the telephone receiver. 'Is that right?'

I knocked on the door. She turned, saw me holding the child and turned back to the phone call. 'I see . . .'

She kept on talking. I felt like shouting at her, running over and grabbing her by the shoulders. Instead, my rage settled to a steel core. I stepped inside.

'I'd better go,' she said into the receiver at last. 'Looks like the kids have been on the road again.'

'I could have run him over,' I said in a voice that didn't sound like mine. 'He was just stepping out . . .'

She took him, reluctantly, into her arms.

'I know, they're terrible,' she said, not catching my eye. 'Soon as I get on the phone they're off.'

'But he could have been killed.'

She looked at me as if she'd heard it a thousand times before. I wondered how many other bewildered motorists had returned her children. Sometimes, my feelings get so intense, my tongue becomes crippled. Maybe I was afraid of losing control, of making a spectacle.

I wanted to tell her what it's like to lose a child on the road. That it's the most horrific experience a parent can endure. To lose a child is to lose hope. If she knew the long, painful years of trying to rebuild a life after such a loss, as I have, the indifference in her eye wouldn't exist.

By the time she's ready to start caring, it may well be too late.

One of the guests at a birthday party I went to recently is associated with a publishing firm. When she announced she had a carton full of books she was happy to hand out, interest sharpened. A cluster of people gathered like fish around a crust of bread.

'What are they about?' someone asked, peeking into the carton.

'Oh, the usual stuff,' she said. 'AIDS, and there's a couple on nuclear war.'

The guests' interest maintained its peak. The perils of the great last blast, whether it will be in our part of the world or Theirs, is obviously still of great interest.

But my mind quickly turned to the real war. The one that runs through our population already like a scythe through a wheatfield. The one that is likely to take your mother, lover or child tomorrow. Yet it's the one we all ignore.

I know about the road war because I lost a son in it four years ago. He went off, not in uniform or with ceremony and brass bands playing, but in shorts and thongs with the sound of summer crickets in his ears. Like many thousands of children, he was obliterated instantaneously on the bitumen.

There was no telegram from the Queen. There are no memorials erected in small towns to the tragedy of people who have died on the roads. No national day set aside so we can remember those who have died not because of territorial aggression between two countries, but because of something as meaningless as technology surpassing our own humanity.

It's not a glamorous war that takes the lives of young men in far-off lands. It has none of the terrifying mysteries of nuclear devastation. It isn't linked to something as glamorous as sex the way AIDS is. So there aren't many books, movies or television shows about it.

Yet ordinary people are cut down every week to add to the nightmare list of statistics so cleanly called the Road Toll.

It is seldom pointed out that when someone you love appears on that list your life is never the same. After a few months, you put on makeup, buy brightly coloured clothes and learn to make cheerful conversation when you don't feel like it.

You owe it to that person to try to make the most of the thing that she or he no longer has: life. But a part of your insides stays cold and numb. It is a sensation, I suspect, that you take to your own grave.

The families of those who have fallen must struggle to stay emotionally and physically intact. But there are no songs about them. People don't like to have their attention drawn to the war that's going on in their own streets. It's more than a little distasteful.

Clouds of happiness

A visitor from another planet wouldn't believe the extent to which we pretend there is no road war. He would find it totally illogical that we can laugh at lemmings, but meekly accept the fact that next week, next year, tomorrow, another chunk of our community will be torn away, sacrificed on the altar of the motorcar.

The main reason we refuse to acknowledge the situation is a tricky one. Every war has an enemy. It's so much simpler when the enemy is a shadowy mass with equally shadowy politics, a bizarre language and a liking for strange foods.

The awful thing about the road war is that the enemy is within ourselves. The boy next door can turn out to be a killer, so can the grandmother in her Japanese hatchback, or the doctor in his BMW.

While safety is still a minor consideration in car design, we will remain our own enemies. When alcohol and driving are partners and there are no compulsory breathalyser barriers outside every pub, we will go on killing ourselves.

While the design of roads and motorways is more concerned with speed than safety, you must be silently thankful every time a member of your household makes it home at night.

Battlefields are always marked with memorials. The scene of every fatal accident should be marked so that every driver who is armed with a car can see the casualties before he adds more to the list.

The books and films on nuclear war and AIDS are no doubt riveting. I can't bring myself to see them. Not when I've known the simple joy of receiving daisies plucked from the grass by a fair-haired boy, and then the astonishing pain of leaving roses on his grave.

14

Dipping into AIDS

THE HAIRDRESSER was a flamboyant young man who certainly knew his way around a head. His scissors worked as if they were operated by a machine.

'Of course, I really should be wearing rubber gloves to do this,' he said with a wry smile.

The salon was brought to a brief but definite halt. Customers looked up sharply from their copies of *Tatler*. Others ran anxious fingers through their perms.

'Of course not,' I said lightly.

Like a flock of birds that has been unnerved by the appearance of a cat, they took a while to settle down. Nobody likes to talk about it, but everyone thinks body fluids these days. I wondered how many would conduct a search for a competent female hairdresser the second they reached the safety of their kitchen telephones.

It wasn't till I paid the bill and got out on the street that a flood of doubts arrived. Perhaps I had taken his remark too lightly. What if he'd snipped just a little too close and caused a minor cut that mingled with the tiny graze on his fingers? Then, assuming he had the virus, what if . . .?

There are two sorts of AIDS. The real thing and Neurotics' AIDS. All the people who used to think they had brain tumours and cancer now suffer Neurotics' AIDS. They get it from swimming pools, toilet seats, dirty towels, unwashed drinking glasses and people breathing over their faces. For every case of real AIDS, there are at least 100 000 neurotic cases.

Let's get sensible about this. Anyone who is informed knows AIDS is hard to get. More people die on the roads.

'Do you know . . .' a friend said over lunch one day. 'There's a smart young executive in town who met a beautiful woman at a party? It was instant attraction. She went back to his place. Next morning, when he woke she was gone. She'd written 'Welcome to the wonderful world of AIDS' in lipstick on his bathroom mirror.'

Another woman at the table had heard the same story. They discussed it in scandalised tones. Two weeks later, I read the same yarn in a foreign newspaper. Apparently, school kids were scaring each other witless with it, creating an ideal breeding ground for Neurotics' AIDS.

It seems incredibly unfair that urban myths still cite the woman as the callous carrier of disease, but I suppose that's beside the point. Even though most people know they can't catch AIDS from drinking glasses, they're terribly fussy. They hang onto the same jar all night. Otherwise they ask for straws or drink straight from the bottle. They haven't worked out you can catch Neurotics' AIDS from anything.

Then there's social kissing. It never was spontaneous. Now it's downright stage-managed. In San Francisco they used to blow kisses, till someone worked out you got Neurotics' AIDS that way.

People assess your AIDS risk on a scale of one to ten before making cheek to cheek contact like Victorian aunts. Frankly, I'm delighted when someone says 'to hell with it' and kisses me on the lips.

It's time to settle down. We all know promiscuity is out and safe sex is essential, but let's stop the siren wailing. Whether we like it or not, we're stuck in this mess called humanity. No matter how hard you try, sooner or later, you'll eat off a fork that hasn't been washed properly, or breathe a molecule of air that's been inside the lungs of a real AIDS sufferer. It won't kill you.

A woman I know went to a party that was full of gay men. She couldn't help being anxious about her glass. She watched it the whole night and made sure no one so much as brushed his coat tail on it.

Next morning, she realised she'd been calming her fears with food. The dip, to be precise. It was a rich, creamy concoction that had worked its way up to body temperature as the night progressed.

Everyone had dabbled crackers, chippies and pieces of vegetable in it. With a ghastly sinking feeling, she realised she too had come down with Neurotics' AIDS.

Dipping into AIDS

It's hard to know if people are sincere when they say 'how are you?' I usually assume they don't want to know at all. They just expect you to make a nice noise back at them.

When life, however, becomes racked with pain, it seems dishonest to say 'fine' when you mean lousy. After several days of agony, I started to admit my wisdom teeth were giving me hell.

The oral surgeon took one look, said 'should have come out fifteen years ago', and made a date for the operation.

'How are you?' someone chirped in the lift on the way back to work.

'Miserable. My wisdom teeth are hurting and I'm having them out next week and I hate operations.'

'Impacted, are they?'

'Yes.'

'Oh, that's terrible. When I had mine out I felt like I'd been run over by two trucks. You'll need weeks off work.'

'The surgeon said five days.'

'Oh, they always underestimate these things. General anaesthetic, is it? . . . But it takes weeks, months even, to recover from one of those. They never tell you, do they? All my hair fell out, too. Did they tell you that?'

She hopped out of the lift like an agile sparrow, caught sight of one of her friends walking past, pointed at me and said, 'Hey, she's having her wisdom teeth out!'

Her friend suddenly put on a funeral director's face and scurried over to help me out the door.

'You poor thing!' he said. 'I've never seen so much blood!'

'Where?' I said, looking anxiously along the corridor.

'At the time I had mine out,' he said. 'My throat was simply full of blood when I came out of the anaesthetic. I thought I was going to choke to death. It was everywhere!'

This was small comfort to a woman who had just received a note titled 'Advice to patients before surgery'. The final paragraph was something about wearing old clothes because sometimes you get blood on them.

'But you'll be right,' he said. 'Have it done late in the day so you can sleep it off all night.'

My appointment was for 9 a.m. I hadn't heard so many scare stories since I was pregnant. I'd always assumed it was a nasty henpecking trait in some women that made them tell you about the time they haemorrhaged all over the kitchen floor and the head got stuck. But when it came to teeth stories, men were even worse.

'There I was lying in the most terrible pain you can imagine,' another said, waving his pen in the air. 'But the anaesthetic hadn't worn off properly and I couldn't tell a soul about it. I must have lain there like that for twenty minutes. Thought my life was over.'

'Then of course,' his mate added, like the second violin in a duo, 'there's the bruising. My face was puffed out to here! And I've got a friend who went black with bruises right down to his neck.'

'Thanks a lot.'

Men, I decided, are cowards. Unaccustomed to blood and the rigours of childbirth, they make the most of physical problems when they turn up. Maybe it's their lack of familiarity with pain that makes them foolish enough to go to wars.

I resolved never to mention the operation again. But word had spread.

'I know someone who had the same thing last Friday,' my roommate said. 'I rang him on Sunday and he still couldn't get out of bed. They cut into the jaw, you know. Right into the bone. If they cut too deep, they sever a nerve and you never feel around the front of your mouth again. I suppose it makes you dribble uncontrollably.'

By the time T-day arrived, I was oddly devoid of fear. If the surgeon had opened the door swinging a butcher's knife, I wouldn't have been surprised. The anaesthetist whistled 'Whistle While You Work' and sent me to that mysterious land between sleep and death.

When I awoke, there was blood, but not too much. Pain, but not unbearable. The front of my mouth was still there. My hair still seemed to be intact and the bill was less than half the quote I'd been given for the same job back in another city.

The nurse handed me the teeth wrapped up in white paper — it seemed a tooth fairy sort of thing to do. The teeth were small to have caused so much trouble. I felt like taking them home and turning them into earrings to terrorise the scaremongers with. But that would not have been wise.

I didn't know it then, but an ear ring of another sort was about to enter my life. I sat back in Elizabeth's comfortable floral armchair and studied the ceiling. Whether it was my third or fourth champagne was hard to tell. She'd kept filling the glass before it was empty. Anyway, who was counting? An empty bottle lay on the floor by her feet.

That was when I heard it the first time. A high-pitched, constant note, not unlike the sound of a clarinet. I studied Elizabeth's face to see if she had noticed it, too. But she was laughing raucously about the way post office tellers apologise about the price of stamps these days.

Maybe it was water in my ears from the swim we'd had earlier that day. I shook my head from side to side, but there was no telltale rattling sound in the eardrums. It had to be the booze. I was appalled that we'd indulged to such an extent it had resulted in physical symptoms. It was only a matter of time before I'd see snakes in her carpet and goblins on the furniture.

'I think I'll have a cup of coffee,' I said loud enough to drown the sound.

'No need to shout,' she said, making her way to the kitchen.

That night, in Elizabeth's luxurious guest room, I went to bed with George Bernard Shaw and Dylan Thomas. But neither of them could make the hum go away. The Dylan Thomas biography said he needed very little to make him drunk. After hardly any more than a whiff of leek liqueur, he'd be storming off to rich relatives to do appalling things on their carpets. No one was surprised when he died horribly and too young.

G. B. Shaw, on the other hand, disapproved of things fleshly and liver pickling. He never had ringing in his ears. He lived long enough to become a media bore.

I wrapped the pillow around my head. The booze should have worn off by now. But that haunting note still echoed through my head. It had to be the onslaught of madness. Virginia Woolf heard voices that drove her to drown herself in a river. Beethoven went bananas with his ears, too. Presumably, his ringing was much more interesting. Otherwise, he'd never have been able to write the Ninth Symphony.

Even when I stuck both fingers in my ears, the sound persisted. Got louder, even. Panic set in. I began to understand the genius of master torturers who use sound to destroy their victim's sanity.

I cast the books to one side, pulled the quilted bedspread to my nose, breathed deeply and tried to relax. The only enemy in this lonely terror, after all, was me. If I nursed myself to sleep, morning would soon appear at the window, fresh and free of distant sirens.

Clouds of happiness

I thrashed into consciousness at 3.47 by the eerie digital clock. The ringing drilled through my chest like a gargoyle's tooth.

It was still there in the morning when I staggered to the bathroom. It was bouncing off the living room walls at afternoon tea. Around six, Elizabeth's husband offered me a drink.

'No thanks. It gives me ringing in the ears,' I said.

'*Ah!*' he nodded wisely under his white eyebrows. 'Blood pressure. I know what it's like. You can't drink if you take the pills, and if you don't take the pills you get ears.'

I tried to seem unruffled, as if I'd heard it all before. However, a new wave of anxiety washed in. I'd never had blood pressure before. Premature old age was setting in. Besides what were the pills and where did you get them? It would have been rude to dash to the phone for a doctor straight away. A discreet call from a phonebox later would have to do.

That night, I took an angry young man to bed. But John Osborne was no help. Loneliness and insanity stretched out before me on the dismal grey carpet of life. Elizabeth popped her head around the corner to say goodnight.

'Have you ever noticed . . .' I said, stroking the sheet in an offhand way. 'A sort of distant ringing sound?'

She paused, no doubt preparing for a belly laugh. She put her head on one side, instead, like a budgie.

'You mean that sort of . . . oooooh?'

'Yes! That's it! Ooooooh!'

'Oh, that's just a tap that's on the blink. The plumber's coming next week.'

15

Pad me on the shoulder, honey

COCKTAIL PARTIES are painful events at the best of times. Nothing is less comfortable than arriving in a brightly lit room full of people you ought to know, but don't.

As if things aren't bad enough already, someone turns up and slaps a label saying 'Introducing' on your chest. At a function I went to the other night the labels showed people's jobs instead of their surnames.

James Lawyer posed sleekly in his three-piece suit and bored his eyes into Brigitte Fashion Model, who wasn't really interested. My own label made me feel somewhat inferior. It said Helen Guest. At least there were several distant relatives I hadn't met before, such as Anne and David Guest.

Olive stones are another problem. Everyone else seems able to eat handfuls of juicy black olives without being left with a single sticky stone. Perhaps they swallow them, or do the latest designer clothes have special pouches in which to store the things? It would take a brave person to present the waitress with a fist of freshly sucked stones to put on her tray with the brie and crackers.

At these ghastly occasions, I always end up spending at least half an hour trying to find hiding places for olive stones. Potplants are good. Ashtrays aren't bad, specially if they're those discreet, pedal-operated boxes that sit on the carpet — but you have to be able to aim straight.

There's something seedy about walking around with olive stones in your pocket. Even worse to have them tumble green and bearded out of your glomesh bag at a crucial moment in three weeks' time.

The loo would be a suitable place, but it's not always easy to find. Besides, that would be letting olive stones rule your life. Other people's empty glasses are a happy hunting ground. Ever since AIDS, no one's been keen on picking up their old glass in case it isn't theirs.

As I was desperately hunting for a receptacle while trying to be polite and interesting at the same time, something else felt wrong. A large part of my anatomy seemed to have dislodged itself from my neck and was heading toward my wrist. It was difficult to tell exactly what was going on because of the long, full sleeves I was wearing.

Whatever was happening was painless, but radical. I noticed people's eyes slipping from my face and 'Introducing' label to my neck and shoulders. Their eyes clouded with doubt, then alarm. But they tried to act as if nothing was happening.

Carelessly, I ran a hand over my elbow to discover a huge pulpy mass lodged there. There seemed to be no blood. I felt strangely asymmetrical and deformed. Yet at the same time, it was as if a weight had been lifted from one of my shoulders. So that was it!

In a flush of embarrassment, I rushed to the nearest bathroom to discover the worst. One of my vast foam shoulder pads had made a bid for independence.

I shoved it back where it belonged, but it flipped backwards to give a look that was more Hunchback of Notre Dame than Joan Collins. Perhaps the answer was to rip the other pad out. At least that way I wouldn't be lopsided. But it was still firmly stitched in place.

My evening jacket offered no help. Naturally, it had shoulder pads, too. When I put it on over the shirt, my shoulders reached up to my ear on one side and only half way up my neck on the other.

Back home, there was a drawer full of other disobedient pads lying like foam rubber gondolas with nowhere to go. Shoulder pads are all very well. They're our way of telling men we can square up to them on any subject. But they're not a pretty sight lying in a drawer. In fact, they're reminiscent of the old 'falsies' women used to enlarge their breasts in the 50s.

When the fashion for false biceps finally fades, the nation will be swamped with discarded foam pads. People will have to form workshops to turn them into useful items like lifejackets for dachshunds, draught stoppers under doors and cushions for gnomes.

In the meantime, we women allow ourselves to look sillier and sillier. Doorways will soon have to be redesigned so that we can get through them. Squadrons of birds will come to perch on our shoulders and a whole generation of kids will grow up thinking their mothers are wrestlers.

The only hope was to slip it back in place, pray for the best and head back to all the fun. But as I made my beaming way toward Henry Tax Consultant, I felt it nudging forwards and down to provide me with the largest left breast in history.

Sometimes, even the simplest female-type activities seem impossible.

The baby has eaten my tube of makeup. That's the way it seems at 7.45 in the morning. I look on the dressing table, in her toy box, on the kitchen floor and in the drawer we put things that have no home. It's nowhere to be found.

There is little point in interrogating the rest of the household. To them the makeup tube is of no greater importance than the toothpaste container. They don't realise that apart from costing more than I care to mention, it represents no less than my self-confidence — for the entire day.

Working mothers can't arrive at work looking as if they've just been scraping goo off the kitchen floor, sewing up underpants and sifting through foul-smelling items in the washing machine. While it's true that's exactly what they usually have been doing, they must never let on.

It's essential that they glide into the office five minutes early looking as if they've spent the last two hours soaking in bath salts, having their necks massaged by Sam Neil. Only that way can they convince the world they're in control of the ferocious juggling display of kids, household and job.

I peer into the mirror and try to convince myself I can get away without it. Paranoid to think anyone takes that much notice anyway. The complexion is pale, uneven and three hours short of sleep.

I decide to compensate with lipstick. Instead of the usual mucky red colour, I go for a sensuous crimson. The effect is dazzling with the yellow jacket.

Makeup is an expensive waste of time. I resent having to wear it. Men don't have to get up ten minutes early to apply mascara and eyeshadow. They wouldn't dream of using moisturiser. Why should I have to cake it on as if it's some sort of defence against ugliness and old age?

Clouds of happiness

I trudge along the streets with nothing between the harsh morning light and me. It's bound to be the one day when someone takes a second look and secretly adds five years to my total.

Maybe I should strike a blow for freedom and appear without a face? Something inside won't allow it. A chemist shop is mercifully open. A woman who is at least twenty years older swoops over to examine the wreckage.

'Hmm, let me see,' she says, peering into the pits and craters of my face. 'What do you usually wear?'

'Something called bronze something, I think.'

She glowers. A woman who takes care of herself has no time for such lack of conviction.

'Bronze shimmer?' she says, drawing a muddy streak down my cheek. 'Oh no! You couldn't wear this till the height of summer. It would give you a line.'

'You mean another one?'

She laughs kindly and says no, she means the line where the makeup ends and the neck begins. Her patience is wearing thinner than the girl in the suntan ad.

'By the way,' she says, 'you really should change the colour of your lipstick. It clashes very badly with that jacket.'

Before I know it, she's darting around the shop like a demented cockatoo, waving lipsticks in the air.

'Orange is all the rage this summer,' she squawks. 'But it's more for the younger girls.'

What does she mean by that? My third decade has hardly dawned. How dare she imply I'm over the hill and possibly even the pill? I want to call an immediate halt to this gruesome charade. But she has taken command.

'I know what I want,' she clucks over her shelf of little boxes. 'But I can't . . . Ah! Here it is!'

She brandishes a mucky red lipstick. Exactly the colour I left at home. I stand helpless as she wipes off the sensuous crimson with a tissue and applies mucky red.

'That's better! You really should take your clothes into account. And now for a little blusher . . .'

'I'm not sure it's me,' I say to the compact full of brown sludge.

'But it's good not to be you,' she says. 'Sometimes.'

She smiles the way they must have smiled over the Space Shuttle when the designs were finished.

Pad me on the shoulder, honey

'There!' she says, packing me off with a bag full of junk. 'So glad you turned up when there was time to do something.'

I choose not to examine the statement too closely. When I reach the office, I rub off as much as possible.

Makeup and padded shoulders aren't women's only troubles. Few men can understand the agony of the pointed toe. If they looked closely enough, however, they'd see how many women have been hobbling around with pain written all over their faces.

Our misery has been compounded by the fact we're supposed to wear four-inch heels the shape of nails as well. Heels that get stuck in manhole covers, between the slats of wooden decking and under the clutch pedals of cars.

These are taxi shoes — made for looking good when you get in and out of taxis, nothing more. I tried to go along with the fashion, but it was killing. Even when I took the shoes off at night, they'd continue to haunt me. I'd wake with throbbing feet and the sensation the shoes were still on.

When I could stand it no longer, I went to a shoe shop. The display of crippling footwear would have done justice to a torture chamber.

'Haven't you got anything for ordinary feet?'

'Sorry, this is the only shape the manufacturers are bringing out this year.'

Not for the first time, I glanced enviously at the men's section. I imagined the uproar if manufacturers offered them anything but wide flat and comfortable.

'But what if I have to run for the bus?'

The shoe shop man shrugged. In a shadowy corner near the fire exit was a small selection of normal-looking shoes.

'Italian,' he said flatly. 'We're not getting any more, so they're half-price.'

It was great to see Italian women still had feet instead of triangular wedges at the bottom of their legs. I slid my foot into the soft leather and was 100 per cent hooked.

As I trudged down the street in the new low-heeled, round-toed shoes, I felt proud to have given up slave-to-fashion status. Life takes on new meaning when your feet don't hurt. I felt calm, in control, free. I almost wanted to stop my teetering sisters and lecture them on the advantages of rebellion. That true emancipation would remain a dream until we women woke up.

Clouds of happiness

A few days later, I was late leaving home for work. A bus appeared on the horizon. It was puffing impatiently as if it was in a hurry. It pulled up at the stop half a block ahead. There was no way I'd catch it unless . . .

The world suddenly turned on edge. I was flying in slow motion through the air and . . . 'Hoomph!'

It was a loud sound accompanied by a sharp exhalation of air. I looked around to see who had made the noise, and realised it must have been me. There was no one else lying face down on the pavement.

My hands were stretched out in front of me — skinned and bleeding on the gravel. My left knee hurt, too.

There are times when the last thing you want to meet is a gallant man. I hoped one wasn't rushing toward this scene to pick up the crumpled piece of person, dust it down and say, 'Are you all right?'

Gallant men are great for picking up handkerchiefs. They're fine for sitting at the end of the bath that's got the taps. They're not bad for snuggling cold feet against in bed. But I prefer them to steer clear of events that involve public humiliation.

As I lay in the watery sunlight for what seemed hours, it became apparent there were no gallant men around. Or even any helpful women. I gathered up the bags and papers that had scattered like shrapnel and tried to pretend nothing had happened.

The woman in the chemist shop was extremely sympathetic. She wouldn't hear of me buying sticking plaster and ointment. Instead, she took me out the back, bathed my hands in disinfectant and dressed them.

'Never run after a bus or a man,' she said. 'That's what they always say, though I don't believe them. If you don't run after a man he's not going to run after you, is he? How did it happen, anyway?'

It can't have been the shoes. They were the level-headed Italian kind. I replayed the events — the bus, panic . . . a big step forward, the beginning of a sprint, then a jarring sensation.

'It was my skirt. I'd forgotten how tight and straight it was.'

The woman laughed.

'You mean you were tripped up by a skirt! Women will do anything to make ourselves attractive. When will we ever get sensible about clothes?'

16

Who's counting, anyway?

I HAVE a confession to make. I never got used to metrics. I can't bring myself to walk into a shop and ask for a size 80 bra. Specially when my waist is 710. If metrics were logical, that would mean I was shaped like a giant egg — a person fit only for display in a circus.

When I was growing up, Mum used to speak wistfully of women with eighteen-inch waists and whalebones. Although I couldn't work out what the skeletons of huge mammals had to do with it, an eighteen-inch waist seemed a modest enough goal. My own waist was sixteen-inches at the time, but no one was impressed. I lived in hope they'd take notice after my eighth birthday.

A foot in those days was reassuringly close to the size of a real foot — a sexist man's foot, naturally. But it was simple enough to make that conversion. A twelve-inch ruler was exactly the right size to fit in your school bag, and flick little screwed-up balls of paper at boys in the front row.

A yard was the size of a stride, or a great leap, depending on your size. Cooking instructions came in cups and teaspoons. It was all wonderfully vague and comfortable.

These days, I feel like someone who escaped from a time machine. The young woman behind the delicatessen counter at the supermarket claims she doesn't know what a pound of cocktail sausages looks like. I'm sure she's having me on when she gingerly puts three on the scales.

A pound of meat, I want to say, is fit for a family of four. It's a handsome amount that sits cosily in two cupped hands. The poor woman seems on the brink of tears as I urge her to place the eighteenth cocktail sausage on the scales.

The fruit shop man is more self-assured.

Clouds of happiness

'You mean 500 grams,' he says in dictator tones when I ask for peaches.

He doesn't seem to realise that food for chickens is the only thing that comes in grams.

If I'm ever forced to buy fabric to make curtains, I expect no cooperation at all from the draper. My only hope is to treat metres as long yards. It always means I have enough fabric left over for matching cushions, lampshades and toilet roll holders.

While metric measures were formalised many years ago, they haven't been a success. The reason is simple enough. Metrics are silly.

When police describe a runaway as being 182 centimetres tall, it means nothing to anyone except a few mathematical geniuses. The man could be a dwarf or a drag queen in six-inch heels (whoever referred to heels or anything else that size in centimetres?)

Metrics are supposed to make things simpler. But like so many inventions of the high-tech era, they've made life more complex. No one can lie like a computer, and few things can confuse as much as a kilometre. Everyone thinks they know how many kilometres it is to the next town, but nobody knows.

Kilometre wasn't a pretty word to add to the language. You can't say people came from kilometres around, or sing I'd walk a million kilometres for one of your smiles.

The new generation of kids was supposed to grow up metric. But our son, who was born at the time of conversion is bilingual when it comes to measures. He operates my old feet and inches camera lens with the flair of someone from the 50s. Yet he talks centimetres at school.

Shoe shops are the only haven left for people like me. I'm still plain old 9½C — an outlandish size that's useful at sale times. Only swanky import shops try to imply there's another way to measure feet. Once they've muttered 'continental fitting', however, they back down gracefully.

If the world was logical, my dresses would be 9½C too. But they're 14, which doesn't have much to do with an 80 bra. The last pair of gloves I bought was an eight and the only hat I own is 7⅛.

When I walk down the street, it seems people don't come in all that many sizes. There are small, medium, large and giant-sized ones. Surely it's time we divided their clothes up into those four sizes and left it at that.

Who's counting, anyway?

In the meantime, I won't believe in metrics till there are ten hours in a day, ten days in a week and ten months in a year.

Sometimes, it seems as if people are too obsessed with the size of things, specially their own bodies. I'm glad Prince Andrew married a girl with freckles and a past. It's a relief to see someone who looks like an ordinary human on the magazine covers.

Sarah Ferguson is the type who laughs, cries, makes mistakes and doesn't always look beautiful in front of the camera. I'm grateful to the palace for allowing the possibility of red-haired grandchildren; overlooking the fact the bride's stepfather is from a country Britain hasn't made peace with yet and accepting the notion that princesses don't have to arrive untouched in cellophane boxes.

But more than anything, I'm delighted the Duchess of York is a normal size. The media has been keen to point out that Sarah is much larger than the Princess of Wales. As they've compared the two women's weights and food intakes, they've implied that Sarah is too fat — a woman who should feel sufficiently ashamed of herself to go on a diet. They'd like Sarah to make excuses, try desperately to 'go off' her food and whittle herself down to a royal skeleton.

People have become so obsessed with the idea that thin is beautiful, they seem to have gone blind. A thin woman may be a great clothes horse, but so are the stick models in shop windows. Take the clothes away and the frame is emaciated, non-sensual and, frankly, boyish.

Although the royals irritate and offend some sectors, their influence soaks deeper than India ink on linen. When Diana burst onto the scene, everyone wanted a haircut like hers, a sapphire engagement ring like hers and a wedding dress with puffed sleeves. Women spent hours staring into mirrors acquiring a round-eyed, wistful look. They even started seeing advantages in men with big ears.

When the Princess of Wales started to get thin, the media said she'd lost her puppy fat and they called her elegant. When she began to look alarmingly thin, she was simply called slender.

These days, her clothes no longer accentuate the undernourished frame. If she eats a plate of spaghetti in public it's news. Yet when her size is compared with Sarah's, we're still left in no doubt. Thin is good, right and best. Normal is . . . well, a bit laughable.

I'm sure the Princess of Wales has the best of medical attention, so there's probably no need to worry about her health. I do, however, worry about the millions of young women who aspire to be like her. She is yet another role model who says curves are dangerous and normal is too fat.

The message is so consistent, so forceful, it's no wonder many young women suffer anorexia nervosa. They become so disappointed and repelled by their own 'imperfect' bodies, they no longer see themselves for what they are.

Research shows that even when they become dreadfully thin, many anorexics believe they look three times fatter than they are. It's good to know these unrealistic assessments can be corrected with help from video cameras. When anorexics see themselves on screen, they must confront the truth.

People often talk about the pressure on adolescents. They have to cope with an onslaught of advertising and violence on television, and come to terms with their own sexuality. They also have to learn that no matter what anyone says, success in this world is to do with winning. Sadly for many young women, winning is still to do with getting the right man. And that, they believe, is to do with being thin.

Recent surveys show that thin women tend to be less happy than their more buxom sisters. Most have endured a considerable struggle to get skinny. Despite their appearances, thin women are notoriously obsessed with food. Their daily calorie intake is their main topic of conversaion — and they can be overtly aggressive toward normal-sized women who eat to feel good and to stay healthy.

It's no surprise that the thin face is so often a sad one. It's even sadder that so many young women take up the deadly habit of smoking simply to get skinny. Magazines and advertisements encourage young women to compare themselves with rake-like models and feel deeply dissatisfied. If only there was another force, equally strong, telling them they're beautiful as they are. That if they eat well, they'll be healthier, more attractive and, ultimately, happier.

I'm delighted Sarah announced to the world that she's pleased with her shape. When the world sniggers at her rounded proportions, it simply demonstrates how unwell we have become.

Who's counting, anyway?

Hers is a womanly, sexy body what would have earned a place on the canvas of any of the great painters in previous centuries. It took the twentieth century to invent the atom bomb, motorway pileups . . . and the myth of the skinny woman.

It's surprising the number of women who spend their time feeling hungry, yet they hold back for the sake of their figures. The chance to let go never seems to come round. But what if . . . ?

The hairdresser can always be relied on for sparkling conversation. Her contacts range from fashion designers to funeral directors. She knows them all, and how many spouses they had before the current one.

'What would you do,' she said the other day, 'if you were told you had only two weeks to live?'

'I don't know,' I said. 'What would you do?'

'I'd eat!' she said, running her tongue over her lips. 'I'd buy an entire sweet shop and guzzle the whole lot.'

'I'd write to that Pakistani cricketer,' the proprietor said. 'You know, the sexy one, and explain the situation. Then I'd hammer on his door. He wouldn't turn me away, not under the circumstances. I'd tell him he could have all the sixteen year olds he liked after the two weeks were up.'

'As long as he was perfectly sure you didn't have AIDS,' the younger assistant said glumly.

The young assistant isn't always easy to recognise. Her hair is a different colour every time I see her. When asked what she would do with her precious two weeks, she leant on her broom and thought a while.

'I'd go out and get a man,' she said. 'I don't want to die a virgin, and I wouldn't have to tell Mum.'

Another client gazed soulfully into the mirror.

'I'd say all the nasty things I've always wanted to tell people — especially my mother-in-law!' she said with an evil smile.

Human bodies are efficient machines, on the whole. There aren't many engines that work for 70-odd years without needing spare parts or major overhauls. Bodies are great, but it's only natural they should wear out after a while.

Most of us have more than two weeks to come to terms with it all. People say you should live every day as if it's your last, but you seldom do. Most of us go to sleep with a bundle of unresolved angers, guilts, ambitions and regrets churning inside our heads.

Clouds of happiness

I learned a lot from my father as he grew older. He seemed to spend the last fifteen years of his life untangling those screwed-up emotions. He became increasingly accepting of the peculiarities of friends and family, and his love of nature and the landscape grew deeper.

Toward the end of his life, he almost became part of the leaves and trees. He would stand alone on a beach or in glistening native bush and drink it all in. He put so much emotion into the enjoyment of a sunset, it was as if it was partly him.

Maybe it's not such a crazy thing to do. Our caveman ancestors undoubtedly experienced the world with similar passion. However, two weeks isn't a long time. As I asked around, I was surprised how many women friends wanted to literally eat the time away. Top restaurants, chocolate, icecream.

'I'd want to taste the best champagne in the world,' said one friend. 'See the best shows and the movies that have meant the most to me.'

Travel was important for most people — except with only two weeks, they didn't want to spend a lot of time in the air. Some wanted to visit countries they considered soul homes — Africa, South America, Greece.

'I just want to go to a safari park and stand among the animals,' another person said.

My son wanted to ride in the back of an F-14, or in the front if he had a pilot's licence.

'I'd want to be on a tropical island with all the people who mean the most to me,' someone else said. 'I wouldn't want to have to draw up a list and invite them. The important ones would know who they were and just be there.'

A party with no booze was another idea, so that people could say how they really felt about each other, without drama or self-pity.

People seemed to have such clear, sensible ways to spend their last fortnight that I began to wonder if everyone should aim to have two weeks set aside in their lives — not necessarily at the end — to do those things.

'But what would you do?' someone asked me.

'If I was told I had only two weeks to live? First I'd break every dish in the house. Then I'd ask for a second opinion.'

17

It wasn't me, it was the waterbed

ALICE GIGGLED hysterically. I knew we shouldn't have come. When she'd asked me to go floating with her, I'd imagined something like a spa pool session. Her bright-eyed terror in the waiting room made it obvious this was something else.

'Do we each get our own pools?' I asked.

'Yes, except they're more like tanks,' she said. 'The water's full of epsom salts, so it's very buoyant and silky and you just lie there floating.'

She has a tendency to get into crazy things, but this sounded harmless enough.

'You just put the lid down . . .' she went on.

'The lid!? You mean you can't get out once you're in?'

'Of course you can. There's a knob on the inside and you can get out any time you like.'

'But what if it gets stuck?'

'They call it sensory deprivation,' she said, ignoring me. 'If you lie there long enough, your mind takes an inward journey towards its own peaceful and undisturbed nature.'

'But what happens if you can't get out?'

'You didn't see that movie called *Altered States*, did you?'

'No.'

'Fine.'

I could tell she had asked me along for moral support. No normal person shuts themselves inside a floating coffin for an hour.

'What does *Altered States* have to do with it anyhow?'

'Oh, the leading man had weird spiritual experiences in one, but he was on drugs and he turned into a gorilla.'

The float house woman sensed our different moods and tried to calm us both down. She handed out sheets of paper explaining the routine. We would each be shown into our own private rooms where we would remove clothes, makeup and jewellery and take a shower.

It was then a matter of putting in ear plugs, covering any cuts and abrasions with the vaseline provided (salt water stings), hopping into the tank, pulling down the lid and floating. Towards the end of an hour, music would be piped through to the tank and it would be time to get out.

'Just enjoy your sensuality,' she said mysteriously.

It's not easy suddenly finding yourself shut in a strange, flesh-coloured room. The white tank gleamed like a space capsule in one corner. In the centre of its roof it had a roll-down hatch that anything could climb out of — Dr Who or a mutated gorilla.

It would have seemed churlish to spend the whole hour in the shower. I grabbed the towel, stuck the plugs in my ears and made a dash for the tank. It was surprisingly shallow inside. No deeper than a paddling pool.

The air was stifling. The water was body temperature, and so slimy, I half-expected to encounter jellyfish. In case something was watching me through a camera and making notes, I lay back in the elastic cradle. My hair stretched out like fingers in the wetness.

The open hatch glared a challenge. I tried to pull it down, but it didn't run smoothly. If it jammed I'd be stuck in there forever, destined to become . . . a shellfish? Who would hear the calls of distress?

I closed my eyes and pretended the hatch was shut.

'This is the silliest thing I've done in my life,' said an internal voice.

A lonely sadness set in. Had humans made life so intolerable on earth they had to shut themselves in plastic containers to find serenity?

I had no weight and the tension eased in my neck. A lot of surface area seemed above water level, and felt cold. If I could shut the hatch properly, I'd warm up. I pulled it down till the outside world was represented by no more than a crack.

Heartbeats thudded in my ears. Breathing came in long, slow heaves from deep in my chest. It seemed an effort to keep functioning. After a while, an extraordinary thing happened. My legs seemed to become lighter than air and rose straight up above my head. They were just about to topple over backwards when I started back into consciousness. After the float, I often wondered where the illusion would have travelled if I'd followed it.

The salts formed crystals around my forehead. Something dribbled into one eye and made it burn so badly I had to keep it shut. The world seemed even further away through one eye.

Time was impossible to judge. Even a breath seemed two minutes, or two hours long. Images drifted past. I was a wet caterpillar in a chrysalis, impatient to burst into the world with wings at last.

A child, at first joyful, then uncomfortable and restless in its womb, longing to get out. Suddenly on the brink of bursting into tears and yelling, I sat up. I'd had enough.

Just when I was composing excuses about why I'd got out early — I couldn't have lasted more than twenty minutes — the music came on.

Despite mixed feelings about the experience, I felt unusually refreshed and energetic that evening. The effect carried through the next day. We hired the video of *Altered States*, too. I'm happy to announce no extra body hair and banana consumption is stable.

Those who can't stomach the thought of locking themselves up for a float can always try sleeping on water every night.

Either we were getting bigger or the bed was getting smaller. Those midnight collisions that used to seem so intimate in the early years of marriage are just a nuisance when you're both exhausted and trying to sleep.

As time went by and our innerspring got more uncomfortable, our friends became high-pressure salespeople. They invented endless excuses to make us lie on their waterbeds.

Things have improved since they brought out the first waveless models. You can actually sit on one side without catapulting your beloved across the room. I dragged my husband and the baby to one of those emporiums that sells waterbeds.

Beds en masse are tacky enough. But when you visit a showroom full of purple draylon and significantly shaped bed-ends, you begin to feel self-conscious and more than a little inadequate. An unusual woman slithered out from behind the counter.

'Would you like to try one?' she said.

My husband blushed. Any moment, he'd turn and run out the door.

'Yes, please,' I said.

She nudged us toward something that looked as if it had belonged to Henry VIII. There was room for him and several of his wives. I peered around the edge of the headboard, almost expecting to find a pair of handcuffs for special occasions.

'Haven't you got something a little plainer?'

She pointed to a colonial masterpiece with cotton reels reaching for the sky.

'We call it "Gone With The Wind".'

She readjusted her sequin-spangled belt as I tried to explain we wanted much plainer. Setting her mouth in a sullen pout, she led us to the Scandinavian section. All pine and rolling in the snow. I began to feel tired. None of them looked as if they were for sleeping in.

She placed a small rubber mat on a model called 'Erik The Red' and urged me to lie on it. The mat, I discovered, was to put my feet on. The bed gurgled with indigestion. I stared up at the shop ceiling and hoped no customers would arrive.

'He has to lie on it too,' she said, glaring at my husband who was holding the baby in self-defence. He put the baby in her pushchair and obliged.

'What do you think?' I muttered. 'It's a bit . . . ostentatious?'

The woman rattled her bangles and leaned over us.

'You can have a fourteen-day free home trial,' she said, slitting her eyes.

'I don't think so,' he said, sitting bolt upright and making the bed belch.

'We've got a hydraulic version out the back.'

My mind boggled.

A small group of people had gathered outside the shop window. They gazed at us with the same blank expression people have when they're watching television.

'Let's go,' he said.

'We'll think about it,' I said to the waterbed woman.

And we did. We decided to try a family department store that would understand the more respectable aspects of bedding.

An elderly man in a grey cardigan and spectacles sailed toward us. We found a waterbed that looked like a conventional one. We said we'd take it because we didn't want to drag around any more shops. His beady eyes roamed over both of us.

It wasn't me, it was the waterbed

'Do you want it tonight?'

'That would be nice.'

He tried to repress an evil cackle. I wanted to say we'd been married for one hundred years and simply wanted some sleep. But that, I suspected, would destroy his fantasy. Going by the flush of pleasure on his face, he'd always dreamed of a couple marching in and demanding a bed immediately. At last, he'd made it come true.

With an operatic gesture, he called the delivery boys out the back.

'These people need a bed . . . tonight!' he announced so the whole shop could hear.

The delivery man looked at my husband with respect verging on awe. Their imagination had already transformed the pushchair into a double deluxe. Dream on.

Waterbeds and float tanks may seem rather affected ways to find relaxation. But anything's worth a try. At least, that's how I felt when I got a pain in the neck.

Nights were worst. I could barely lift my head off the pillow. Every time I tried to turn over, it was total pain. I'd have to move the rest of me to see if my neck would agree to follow. Sometimes, it wouldn't.

Other times, in the depths of the night, the pain crept right down my arm to a spot between my first and second fingers. On the bus home after work, the neck felt every lump, bump and drain lid on the road.

Standing up was dreadful. Sitting, no better. Lying down was sheer agony. Something had to be done. I needed instant relief. Something short, sharp and permanent. For some reason, the sign I walked under during most lunch hours came into focus. It said ACUPUNCTURE in big yellow letters.

I flicked through the yellow pages. The acupuncture section was full of dragons, Chinese writing and people with inscrutable letters after their names. They offered cures for everything from sporting injuries and haemorrhoids to smoking and facial tics. There had to be something in it for a sore neck.

One claimed to use painless non-needle acupuncture. He was out. Did this mean that ordinary acupuncture involved pain? I tried the next one on the list. A heavily Oriental voice answered the phone.

Clouds of happiness

'How you spell your name? D-r-o-w-n?'

As the taxi laboured up the hill to his rooms, I imagined needles the size of road drills driving into my neck.

'S'pose you've tried all the proper doctors?' the driver said, handing me the change.

A Chinese woman in her 50s greeted me at the reception desk. She was reading a recipe book for European cooking.

'Will it hurt?'

'No,' she laughed, vaguely. 'Do not be afraid.'

A patient emerged. She was glowing, as if she'd just run around the block — or escaped a nasty experience? I heard the hissing of an aerosol can in the next room. The receptionist said I could go through now.

I walked into a wall of Citrus Grove to find a bespectacled young man sitting behind a desk. His features were mild. He took my pulse — both hands — and wrote a lot of Chinese lettering on his pad. He said the blood pressure was very healthy.

'Will it hurt?' I asked again.

'Do not be afraid.'

I removed my blouse and arranged myself face down on his couch. He ran a buzzing machine over my neck and shoulders. The noise seemed to tell him where the trouble was.

'I will now give you treatment,' he said, turning the radio on to relax me. It was a programme about terminal illness.

The first stab was short and sharp behind my ear. I waited for the next — in my neck. The third landed in my shoulder. The jabs felt like fountain pen nibs on impact. But once they were in, I couldn't feel them.

'I will now give you laser treatment,' he said. 'Close your eyes.'

Partly due to nerves, I misheard him and wondered how fast a woman could run from his surgery half-naked with three needles and a razor in her back.

It turned out to be a machine that gave out deep but gentle warmth. He then removed the needles and showed me four bamboo tubes, teacup sized and harmless looking.

I heard a cigarette lighter flick, a slight smell of burning then, POW! The bamboo cups landed one after the other on my neck. The vacuums inside them sucked up the skin quite savagely. After a while, it dulled to the sort of burning surface pain that makes you think it's doing you good.

It wasn't me, it was the waterbed

Next came something that felt like a mechanical wire brush, followed by a run-of-the-mill machine massage. By the time he was giving me a final neck massage with firm and practised fingers, I realised I hadn't felt so relaxed for months.

I was so relaxed as I headed out the door, I walked into another office by mistake. A dark-suited businessman was hunched over his calculator, looking so tense and unhappy I wanted to tell him to go next door. But I turned and left.

18

The rat who jumped over the moon

'THEY BATH kittens, don't they?'

I wasn't expecting an answer from the pet shop person. It had just seemed an appropriate noise of despair to make while staring at her display of flea powders. None of them had seemed to work.

I'm not obsessive about cleanliness, but I draw the line at small hopping things. They had arrived in the house about the same time as the small black kitten.

'Of course you can!' the woman said.

'In water?'

I examined her face. She wasn't having me on.

'I breed cats,' she said. 'My kittens have always had two baths by the time they go to new homes.'

I bought a can of potent-looking stuff and stored her information near the back of my mental filing cabinet. Pet shop owners have idiosyncrasies on account of preferring animals to people.

The kitten was no ordinary beast. For a start, her mother was thoroughbred and would have been worth one hundred dollars, if she'd had her papers. Admittedly, the father was a mongrel with upmarket taste who lurked in the bamboos. But a little breeding goes a long way.

More importantly, and somewhat terrifying, the kitten had been given to us by a dear friend with the understanding it would be cherished and adored for all its nine lives.

When it all boiled down, a kitten was a kitten. It needed dirt boxes, worm medicine and insect powder. It also liked to be fed. So did other people.

I was flat out one evening trying to zap up a high-fibre feast for two-legged appetites when the kitten started meowing piteously around my feet. A person in normal circumstances would probably have taken it in her stride. But frankly, I find cooking a stressful occupation. It's an unrewarding art form. Even Picasso would have found it hard slaving over a masterpiece knowing the greatest appreciation he could hope for would be a loud, watery belch.

The kitten had no reason to complain while I was boiling up the bran. She had been fed, cuddled, talked to. She was fretting for a mystery. I tripped over her on the way to the fridge. When I opened the door for yoghurt, she sprang into the vegetable crisper.

That was when it hit me like a price rise. It was quite simple. There was only one thing she hadn't had. A bath. I scooped up the small dark bundle and swept into the bathroom.

She watched the water tumbling into the basin as if she expected goldfish to spring from the taps at any second. Obviously, she had never regarded water as something you get into.

I held her firmly, lowered her with speed and dignity, then rubbed shampoo in her wet fur. At first, I was astonished at how placidly she stood there, fur slicked down, looking like a rat gone wrong. I was misreading the signs. She was, in fact, paralysed, woken from an inconceivable nightmare to find it was real. I felt her muscles tense, then all of a sudden she let out a primaeval yowl. Then she went limp.

I lifted the little creature out of the water. Her head and feet swung lifelessly. In spite of my horror, I couldn't help noticing how much she resembled the fox fur stole my mother used to wear.

Something had to be done. Fast. I wrapped her in a towel and ran through to the living room fire, rubbing her frantically and apologising profusely. When I got to the part where I promised I'd never bath her again, she let out a single demure sneeze. I felt a shudder of life through her body. A second later, an indignant ball of wet wool was sitting on my knee licking my fingers as if I'd done her a favour.

The small hopping things have gone. But if they come back, I'll stick to the stuff in cans.

As the kitten grew older, she began to lose that helpless air. She started to specialise in cruelty.

Canned meat and cooked chicken hold no magic for Cleo. She prefers livestock. Blowflies and beetles vanish after two or three crackling crunches. Lizards take longer.

She prowls the garden like a tiny black panther to catch a mouse or bird. She hurtles inside with the poor creatures to butcher them by degrees in what has become her favourite death chamber — our bedroom. It doesn't do wonders for the lovelife.

I'm not heavily into murder. Much as I love sleek little Cleo, her habits revolt me. I wasn't looking forward to the day she would bring in a rat. Most animals I can cope with. Spiders and cockroaches are fine. I even looked at a snake in a zoo, once. The sight of a rat, however, reduces me to jelly.

That night, as I was ironing a dress to go to a movie, loud screeching noises came from the bedroom. That man always reverts to a choirboy under stress.

'I've got bad news,' he said. 'The cat had a rat, but it's all right. I've chased it out.'

'The rat?'

'No, the cat! Don't panic!'

He went outside, collected the cat and threw it back in the bedroom with the rat. I shut myself in another room and turned the radio up.

'They're in the hall now,' he called through the door. 'The rat's climbing up a wire. Only Cleo's lost interest, mainly because the rat's bigger than she is.'

'Can't you do something?!'

'This is like a B-grade movie,' a young male voice said. 'I don't believe it!'

It was the babysitter. He was irritatingly calm.

'All you have to do is drop a bowl over the rat and slide a sheet of cardboard underneath.'

'You can come out now,' my husband said. 'It's disappeared. Must have gone out the front door.'

We left late for the movie.

'No rat?' I said to the sitter when we returned.

None. Next night, when we were watching television, my husband said in an ultra-calm voice, 'You're not going to believe this. I just saw the rat peep out from behind the sofa. Where's the hammer?'

I shot into the kitchen. He ran in after me demanding a hammer. I handed him an orange plastic bowl.

Soon after, he was standing in the night at the bottom of the garden. Three mysterious shapes sailed into the sky. One bowl, one rat and the cardboard cover of a record titled 'Solid Gold Hits Volume 14.'

It's bad enough looking after your own animals. But when other people's elderly relatives move in, I reckon I'm entitled to move out.

The neighbours have gone to Disneyland. So Algernon has come to our place. Not that we really mind. He's a large, ancient fellow of extreme sensitivity. Deep down, he can't understand why he wasn't allowed to go to Disneyland, too.

Some people moved into his house to look after him. But they haven't got a family. Life for Algernon is pale and bleak without kids. He's a grandfather figure. No longer able to participate in their more hectic games, he spends a lot of time standing around with a broad smile on his face. His joints are stiff and slow, so he gets in the way a lot. He's likely to collect a sharp crack on the back in 'bullrush', but he knows nobody does it on purpose.

Kids don't tease him much because there's nothing they like more than an audience. Algernon always approves. Predictably, adults are less tolerant. They regard him as socially unacceptable. Not just because he hangs around kids. Or the fact he's no longer debonair.

It's more to do with failing muscular control. In short, Algernon is likely to smell. It usually happens when conversation has reached philosophical heights. He tries to pretend someone else is responsible, but it's unmistakable.

'Oh, Alge!' one of his more intimate acquaintances will say.

He'll look hurt and silently retire. When they left for Disneyland, he stood outside their gate, dumbfounded. A few hours later, he was on our doorstep. It was impossible to reject someone so emotionally torn.

But soon the house was overflowing with Algernon, in more ways than one. Everywhere I wanted to go, it seemed he'd arrived there a second before.

'Couldn't we get rid of him in a nice way?' I whispered to my husband.

'Just you try.'

I viewed the possibility of spending the next four weeks manoeuvring life around Algernon with feelings best described as mixed.

'He's a nice enough old thing, but where would he sleep?' I said. 'And what about the . . . ?'

'I suppose we could keep the windows open.'

I went to the living room where Algernon was dozing in the full blast of the fire.

'Look, I'm sorry, but we're having dinner now.'

He lifted his head so I could study his reproachful, bleary eyes.

'Sorry old boy, but good night,' I said in my social worker's voice.

He skulked miserably down the path. I, the wicked queen, ugly stepsister and Witch of the West, sat down to the meal, which I didn't enjoy.

All he'd wanted was reassurance that his world hadn't dissolved altogether.

'That's the trouble with life today,' my husband said. 'Nobody's prepared to accept responsibility for the elderly.'

I looked up from my plate and saw a ghostly face at the dining room window. It stared, unblinking, at me. Algernon was back. My husband scraped back his chair and went to the door.

'But if we start feeding him, we'll be stuck with him,' I said.

'Oh, all right. Go home, Alge!'

But he stood there wearing that accusing stare.

I was toying with my salad when a strange sound filled the air. It started as a sort of cough and built to a dreadful moan.

'He's crying!'

'For heaven's sake, let him in!' I said.

Algernon tottered in the door, let out his tongue and gave me a generous lick on the knee as he went past. We looked at each other and smiled. There was no need for words. We both knew it was a cruel trick of nature that had trapped Algernon in a fur-covered, four-legged body.

19

Roman circus

AS SOON as you give birth to a kid, you realise you're going to make a lot of sacrifices. The first one is sleep. You forget how it feels to let your nerve endings wake up of their own accord.

Sometimes, you become conscious halfway down the hallway en route to a crying bassinet. On other occasions, you're likely to be staggering off, rosehip bottle in hand, after a yowling cat.

Conversation also goes out the window. For the next fifteen years, it will be impossible to talk to anyone in full sentences. 'Don't do that or I'll . . .' and 'Because I said so' become your theme songs.

But of all parental sacrifices, the most noble and demanding is the merry-go-round.

'Look!' she said as we ate our lunch of hot dogs, popcorn and cordial laughingly described as bottled juice.

'Yes, that's the merry-go-round. We might go on it later.'

The 10 year old had already vanished to have his thirty-sixth ride on the dodgems. She waved her frankfurter dispiritedly in the air. I couldn't blame her for not eating it. You could almost taste the additives.

'Mewwyground,' she said in the voice they know parents can't resist.

I followed her sturdy, running legs to the queue. Merry-go-rounds belong to a more gracious era when things stopped and started slowly. Today's ZAP! POW! kids were impatient by the time it ground to a halt.

It says a lot for the design that something invented so long ago — before computer games and rockets — can still attract kids. There's undoubted magic in the garish colours, the diamond-shaped mirrors and the organ box 'Blue Danube' music.

She was too young to go on it alone. I would have to go, too —

not as a rider, but an accomplice, standing beside her gyrating horse, making sure she didn't fall off. The thought wasn't appealing to someone prone to seasickness.

Just the night before, I'd seen the world's most horrific roller coaster on television. The passengers were strapped into standing position. I figured being vertical on a merry-go-round wasn't much better.

Merry-go-round horses are like poeple. You can't find the perfect one. They either have stirrups, but no tails, or they're prettily painted with one stirrup missing and a grey string for a tail.

In the rush for horses, I steered her toward one on the inner side of the circle, in the hope that centrifugal force would work in our favour. She grabbed the chromium pole and a satisfied smile set on her lips. I clutched her saddle and waited.

Two roughly dressed teenagers, cigarettes in hand, straddled the horses in front of us to experience the childhood they'd never had.

Once a merry-go-round gets started, it stops for no one. The operator is blind to the green-faced parent who clings to her child as the world goes up and down and round and round.

It's not helpful to focus on the rapidly spinning fairground. The hot dog stand, the roller coaster, the ticket box blur into a horrific mural of movement.

How could the row of pale faces waiting for their turn possibly watch us with envy? I concentrated on something closer, the horse's orange mane with 'punk' scratched into the paint, to control the urge to scream.

The child started squirming and reached for the empty horse next to hers. It was a crazy time to go for a horse of a different colour, but she was determined. The music played on, cheerfully oblivious, as I tried to lift her onto the new horse. It was up when the old horse was down, and down when the old horse was up.

I was regretting the hot dog, and the icecream we'd had earlier. Would the operator stop this deranged contraption if I threw up? I doubted it.

She got bored with that horse, too, and wanted to try all the others. Eventually, she decided to stand beside me, holding hands as the world spun past. Maybe she was feeling off colour, too.

It was all I could do to stop cheering as it drifted to an end. Knees trembling, I headed for the sanity of a still world. But a small, chubby hand pulled me back. I looked down at a solemn face.

'Again,' she said.

It took two more rides before she was satisfied.

It takes something a little more elaborate to impress a ten-year-old boy.

The roar of a hundred outraged beasts echoed in the distance.

'The sound of glory!' he said as we made our way to the stadium. 'Hurry up! Run!'

There's nothing cultivated about stock cars. People go for the same reason crowds thronged to Roman arenas. Danger, aggression, courage — and maybe even some blood spilt on the dust.

They're hardly cars at all. There's a memory of a Morris 1100 about the rear end of some of them. The rest is part bulldozer, part rocket — made all the more zany by the outlandish wind foils that sit like metallic butterflies on their roofs.

'It's a poor man's speedway,' said the friend who met me at the gates. She could tell I was none the wiser. 'Just choose a car and follow it round.'

No. 37, a ferocious purple vehicle, revved aggressively and nudged the car in front of him in the lap before the race began. He had to be a winner.

'They're not supposed to do that before the race,' my friend said. 'Or during it, for that matter.'

But they do. Helmeted like knights inside their armoured cars, they have to turn on some rough stuff. If they didn't whack and slam into each other in showers of blue sparks, we'd all be disappointed.

I was pleased to see such hair-raising driving contained to a public track. If only all aggressive male drivers would stick to stock cars.

The peppery smell of racing gas tickled our nostrils as the race hotted up. An elegant white number started at the back — and stayed there in every race he entered. It was as if his own performance was a personal affair — or maybe he was hoping the others would all break down.

Two cars got locked together, bullbar to bullbar. They shook angrily, trying to get free, but they stayed locked in reluctant matrimony for the best part of a lap.

No. 37 had become too fierce for his own good. After a series of battles, he whirred into the centre field and expired on collapsed wheels. It's a humbling experience watching your knight being carried off by a gleaming, flashing tow truck.

'He'll be back next week,' someone said.

Amazingly, he was back after a few more races. Rule number one: Stock car men never give up.

The french fried-scented crowd let out a roar of horror when a red car did a complete somersault, landing back square on its wheels. The driver sat stunned for a moment and raised his hand to his face. Crewmen ran over to help, but (rule number two) stock car men aren't sissies. They stood back respectfully as he pulled into the centrefield.

A wheel shot off a souped-up mini, sailed metres into the air and landed in the pits. The crowd strained to see, but misfortune wasn't dressed to kill that night.

'I saw a man crushed to death that way once,' someone said.

Another car lost a back wheel that refused to lose the race. It spun on alone around half a lap, leaving the dilapidated vehicle stranded back down the track.

As the night progressed, the moon rose like a broken biscuit in the sky. Dust coated our hair and clothing like talcum powder.

I thought no one but a handful of suicidal fools would go in the final event, the demolition derby. But one hundred and twenty-five cars in various stages of decay tottered into the ring for their last fight.

An old Holden station wagon had been done up to look like an ambulance. Another car was in traffic cop colours. There were two bright pink Bambinas and several large black things with sharks' fins on their roofs.

It took nearly half an hour for this motley congregation to position themselves for the start — and the same time for them to smash each other into oblivion.

Around midnight, the place looked like a fly killer advertisement. One hundred and twenty car corpses lay dead on the arena. Just when you thought one had expired, it emitted a feeble buzz to let you know it was still hoping. It was a massive scene of destruction. Someone said a Vanguard had won the one thousand dollar prize. But who could tell?

'Don't go so fast,' he said as we hurried back to the car park to check mine hadn't been put in the demolition derby by mistake.

Roman circus

It's a shame about the Romans. If they'd had stock cars, a lot of Christians, slaves and wild animals would have lived a lot longer. It would be interesting to know what those ancient fellows would have made of one of our modern circuses.

Other people cry at weddings. I cry at the circus. There's something remarkably poignant about people who have devoted their lives to entertaining others. In a circus, there are no camera tricks or stand-in stunt men. It's simply them and us.

It's touchingly uncomplicated. They present their best. All we can offer in return is applause. The whole thing seems trivial, yet it's essential to some people's sanity.

Maybe that's why tears are dripping off my chin as I stare up at the trapeze artists from Mexico. Their bodies are small, compact and almost dumpy. Yet here they are pretending to be birds.

What makes a Mexican boy stand out in an impoverished crowd? His looks, or the fact he can soar through the air in white tights and a glitter belt?

The only man in the world to perform a triple flip blindfolded, says the compere. The artist swoops off with a hood over his head. But the seconds split the wrong way. The catcher loses his grip. A single gasp of horror as the star plummets into the net.

'They do it on purpose,' says my friend who has been known to weep at Walt Disney movies. 'To keep the tension up.'

I glance into her cynical eyes. She's got to be wrong. Next time, thank God, he makes it.

'You really are a sucker,' she says when the man on the tightrope loses his balance, drops his skipping rope and nearly falls into the crowd (he has no safety net). 'He's faking.'

Some of the audience have grim faces and cross arms and don't seem too happy about the chimps. The trainer has them dressed in sneakers and tracksuits to parody humanity. Yet they have leads on their collars, like dogs. No monkey in his right mind wants to smoke and pull faces like a person.

It's best to hope they've forgotton their real home among the glossy leaves of the jungle. Or is it? I clap loud because the chimps seem to want it.

There aren't many times in your life when someone catches your eye and you curl up inside like a dried pea. The prisoner in his cage and the black man in South Africa no doubt have the power to do it.

121

So, surprisingly, does the chimp. Her morose stare bores right through me. The eye is disillusioned, accusing, as if it belongs to a broken escapee from a home for the subnormal. I will her to stop.

The clown tries to milk applause. But the audience is an unwilling goat. He's too demanding for approval of his mostly quaint jokes.

The men from Morocco tumble in and fill the tent with good humour and effervescent masculinity. They haven't even been boozing. They leap about and flip like children's toys.

'If there's a heaven, maybe they'll have a troupe like this to meet me,' I whisper to my friend, who rearranges herself primly on her seat.

Overcome by their energy and roguish good looks, I let out a cheer. A particularly handsome one waves back in hearty recognition — to my friend.

The Chinese acrobats are, for me, the highlight. In a semi-hypnotic state, two men climb to the top of a stack of chairs and balance against each other in outlandish positions. The concentration is so intense, the trust so intimate and complete, it's like witnessing a couple in the act of love.

'How come it smells as if there are elephants when there aren't any?' I say to my friend on the way out, to demonstrate how down-to-earth I am about circuses.

She laughs and we walk home trailing a streamer.

20
Booked up

THE BOOK on her counter was titled *How To Complain and Win*. It seemed an unusual book to keep in a library, but I suppose if it was going to be kept anywhere . . .

The librarian in huge spectacles was talking on the phone beside the book. Someone wanted an obscure historic photo from an obscure historic publication.

'Just a moment,' she said. 'I'll look in the stack room.'

I don't mean to sound unreasonable, but I do get irritated when phone calls get priority over people who have taken the trouble to turn up in the flesh.

Another librarian emerged from the back room. And another. They studiously avoided my eye. The first librarian eventually got off the phone and blinked when I asked for a particular book.

'It should be over there,' she said, waving at the horizon.

'I've looked and it isn't,' I said.

She punched her computer and said she'd have to go down to the stacks. To fill in time, I wandered up and down the aisles. I have a friend who decided to read his entire suburban library. He started at A, got as far as G, hooked on Graham Greene, and could go no further.

The librarian reappeared holding the book victoriously.

'But you can't take it out. It's reference only.'

I tried to explain I needed one to take away so I could research an article.

'Take this note to the Social Science desk downstairs. They might have a lending copy.'

I have felt ruffled in libraries before. I was determined not to let it happen again. The Social Science desk was empty, as it had been the past two times I'd visited the library. Several metres away, two women were slaving over microfiche machines. They both wore glasses and were trying so hard not to be noticed. I assumed they were librarians.

'Oh, no dear,' they crowed.

A hawk-like woman with a thousand gold necklaces picked up my note in one claw and said, 'It's in the basement', as she flew past. 'I'll send someone down.'

To keep calm, I picked up a copy of *Ms* magazine and read that Marilyn Monroe would be running a home for stray animals if she was alive and well today. She once took a cow inside to keep it out of the rain.

'Here you are,' said a lesser librarian, handing me the book.

All I had to do now was join the library so I could get the thing out. I went over to the new members' desk.

'Have you belonged to a library in this town before?' said the young woman in a pink fluffy jersey. 'Where do you live?'

As I told her nothing but the truth, I ruffled through my bag for the endless cards and licences that are called identification.

'I'm afraid that's not good enough,' she chirped. 'We need to see a piece of mail with your address on it.'

'What?'

'Have you got a letter in there?'

There seemed little point in explaining that I keep letters at home where they are sent to me.

'Well, I'm afraid you can't join,' she said, drumming her fingers on her computer.

'Isn't there a form I could start to fill in?' I asked hopefully.

'I do all that and it all goes directly on the computer,' she said. 'You'll have to take the book over there and she'll keep it for you till you come back with positive identification of your address.'

The young woman in the fluffy jersey and aqua eyeshadow seemed unaware how close I was to committing librarianicide.

'But I need this book today.'

'You could go to your bank and ask for a printout with your address on it.'

When I thrust the book at the keeper and stormed out the door I was so furious I was planning to move house the next day to make sure the library had the wrong address.

I tried to hide my rage with a sardonic smile when I returned and placed the bank printout under the fluffy librarian's nose. She eyed the slip suspiciously.

'What's your christian name?'

I told her through clenched teeth.

'Well, how come it says Mr and Mrs S. Brown on here?'

I drew a breath.

'Because the world is a very sexist place.'

She must have sensed her luck was running thin. Reluctantly, she wrote out a temporary card for me. When the keeper handed me the book I'd fought so hard for, I was almost quivering with emotion.

'That card is valid for only two weeks,' she snapped. 'You *must* come back here to collect your new card.'

There are times when mass murder seems a viable alternative. One thing's certain. When I do go back, it will be to collect *How To Complain and Win*.

There are, however, times when complaining, no matter how eloquently, is likely to get you nowhere.

Most nights of your life there's a degree of choice in whom you sleep with. He or she might not be ideal, but at least you made a decision to endure each other's peculiar habits somewhere along the line.

The large lady in sunglasses laughed with the guard. The sound echoed through the pillars of the railway station and reminded me of horses. I pitied whoever had to sleep with her on the train. She was obviously a dominant type who would sit by the window and demand conversation. And that laugh!

The baby suddenly decided she didn't want me to go. I hooked her under the arm that wasn't carrying a bag and tried to explain I'd be back in a few days. Babies never believe you.

The woman and the guard grew more hearty by the second. They rolled their lips back and exposed their teeth to the evening light. I had to interrupt because I wanted to find my sleeping berth, and get the goodbyes over and done with.

'Hmm,' the guard said, running a pencil over his list. 'You two ladies are together.'

We looked at each other, horrified.

'Not a *baby*!' she said.

When I explained the baby was staying behind, the woman seemed only slightly relieved. I staggered off to the tiny sleeping compartment that was already choking with her luggage.

When she found the room overflowing with my family farewell, she hovered in the corridor. I could tell she thought they'd stay on the train too long and the five of us would end up sharing this sardine tin on wheels for the next twelve hours.

'How come you're always having fun?' said the ten year old, staring glumly at the sink in the corner.

The baby perched expectantly on the seat and bellowed when she was swept off and back to the car.

My companion agreed to put some of her boxes in the guard's van. That left a mere two suitcases, two overnight bags and a red spiked umbrella to fit around our feet. While she was away, I hastily set up camp by the window and slipped a book from my bag.

I'd put a lot of thought into my reading material. The first was a glorified comic book by a European woman cartoonist. I'd figured short blasts of wit would fill in off moments like now, while we were waiting for the train to take off.

The other, a Real Read, still lurked in the safe shadows of my bag. *The Life and Loves of a She Devil*, by Fay Weldon. I was looking forward to it with the relish of a gourmet's anticipation of frogs' legs in butter.

The door burst open. My partner appeared and flung herself on the seat.

'Dammit!' she said as we glided out of the station. 'Haven't got a thing to read. Not even a newspaper.'

That's when I did something stupid. Whether it was because of a particularly sharp joke in the cartoon book, or because I was relieved she wanted to read rather than talk, it's hard to know. Like a prize fool, I bent over my bag and handed her *The Life and Loves of a She Devil*.

'I suppose you've read it?' I said hopefully.

'No,' she said, turning it over in her hand with too much interest. 'Have you read all her books?'

'No.' I was beginning to worry. 'She's a bit on the dour side, don't you think?'

But my sleeping partner didn't answer. She was already engrossed in page one. As we chunkered out through the suburbs, my companion chuckled over my book while I stared at the increasingly less funny cartoons on my lap.

When she took *She Devil* with her to the dining car, my mouth set in a line. The cartoon book was no longer amusing. It was downright dull.

'This is a funny book,' I said, offering her the cartoons when she got back.

She stared at them for a few seconds. A confused expression clouded her face before she handed it back.

After the steward made up our bunks, she lay above me and cackled till after midnight. Sometimes, in my jolting, restless sleep, I imagined she had grown four moles, pinned me to the floor with her red umbrella and smothered me to death with the cartoon book.

'How did you sleep?' I said from under my pillow at 6 a.m. My mouth had become lizard skin.

'Great!' said the voice above me. 'That was one of my blow-out reads.'

I peered out the window over the empty landscape. We seemed to have arrived in Siberia.

'I want to discuss the ending with you,' she said.

'But I haven't read it.'

'I'll tell you the ending, then you tell me what you think.'

'But I won't be able to read it if I know how it ends.'

'But there are some discrepancies . . .'

'Sorry,' I said, tripping over the umbrella on my way to the sink in the corner.

As she handed back the book, a line of frustration settled on her brow.

MORAL: A she devil in the hand is worth two in a sleeper.

I thought it would be nice to take something home from the book sale for my son. He has unusual tastes. I've bought him books a boy his age should like — adventure stories and outdoor annuals — only to have them put aside after a restrained thanks. Such events are sad, wasteful and mutually embarrassing. I try to avoid them by providing him with stuff he'll read.

'Have you got any books on planes that kill people?' I asked the bespectacled shop assistant.

'I beg your pardon?' The blood seemed to have drained from her face.

'Oh, it's not me. My son reads them.'

She drew herself another inch taller and her eyes became

hooded and steely. Like a person sinking in quicksand, I realised the situation was unlikely to improve. I had encountered a purist who believes parents should restrict their children's reading to Tolkien.

'I can hardly say I approve,' she said coldly. 'My son collects dinosaur books.'

'I've tried him on those,' I said. 'I even bought him a dinosaur press-out mobile, but he never got around to making it. He was too busy gluing Spitfires.'

'Well, I'll have a look,' she said without enthusiasm.

The woman was beginning to annoy me. If she disapproved so strongly of books on planes that kill people, why didn't she give up her job and work in a pet shop?

I wandered over to a huge glossy display of fighting planes in the section called Military. But they were all full price. Books on planes that kill people are popular. That's why they don't get reduced very often.

As I drifted on to the stacks of remaindered books, it became clear that there are plenty of subjects that people don't want to read about. There wasn't, for example, a great market for *The Garden Pest Book*. While its publisher might have imagined it had huge potential, most buyers seemed to have shied off buying it for Dad for Christmas.

The author of *The Illustrated Guide to Glass* probably never thought his creation would end up in a morose stack of leftovers, either. He would have driven the possibility from his head as he sat down to write the first hopeful paragraph.

It looked as if several publishers were taken in when enthusiastic writers burst into their offices and said, 'Have I got a great idea for you! How about a vegetarian cookbook?!'

That sales pitch resulted in the most heavily represented topic in the remainder sale. Vegetarians don't need cookbooks. There's not a lot you can do with raw cabbage and peanuts.

Healthy Desserts was another bummer. When people want pudding, they want high-fat, disgusting goo that's going to make them guilty about destroying their bodies. Nobody wrote an ode to low-cholesterol cake iced with live yoghurt.

It's hard not to be sorry for the publishers and well-meaning writers who gave birth to these slightly unwanted works. Like children, books are conceived with hope and delight. No one wants them to end up spotty and half price.

However, the firm which willingly produced *The Frank Sinatra Scrap Book* deserves public humiliation among the remainders. Who wants a record of one of the world's ten least lovable men? The creators of a modest volume titled *Cricket Skills* are entitled to a little sympathy. The topic is noble and serious. Too bad for them that cricket isn't like soft porn, where the pleasure of reading about it has the reputation of being almost as good as taking an active part.

There's no doubt that a pop-up book about the universe was a great idea. Maybe it was the public's fault that they couldn't see the point of a cardboard solar system. *The 1987 Almanac* doesn't have a great following this year, either.

Feminists will be delighted that *A Gentleman's Relish — A Saucy Look At The Fairer Sex* is going cheap. But they can't comfortably claim victory when *Sexist Society* is reduced on the same stand.

Maybe it's a sign of national maturity that *Sexual Secrets — The Nationwide Report On Love and Marriage* is remaindered. But perhaps our secrets are too dull to be worth knowing. Just when I was about to open the book to find out, the saleswoman reappeared. Her glare was enough to make me blush and put it shamefacedly back on the shelf.

'We have this . . . and this,' she said, handing me two books.

One was about ships that kill people. The other was about planes that don't. I turned them over carefully.

'Have you got anything on dinosaurs in the sale?' I asked.

21

When did he get so tall?

IT HAPPENS only a few times in your life. You run your fingers through the hair on his back and gaze into his liquid eyes. For just a moment, a surge of emotion negates all logic.

You know what you're about to say will commit you to years of drudge, humiliation and stains on the carpet. But there's something hypnotic about the look in his eyes.

If you turn back now, you may never again experience this concoction of bravado and plain stupidity. In the passion of the moment, you hear yourself say, 'Let's have a puppy.'

It's many years since the puppy arrived. We bought her to keep our first child company, seeing we weren't planning any more for a long time. She was a delightful bundle of white fluff with teeth sharper than needles, and a desire to eat anything from underwear to butter.

The child seemed to like the puppy. They were at a similar stage of development. Neither was continent. In moments of intimacy, he would lie across the puppy's stomach to drink his bottles.

Around that time, the Noriday pill factory in Surrey turned out a dud batch. My husband was mowing the lawn with the dog and the child the day I came home from the doctor's and burst into tears. It felt as if the rest of my life would be spent mopping up after babies and dogs.

The dog was fond of the new baby. She peered earnestly into its cocoon-like blankets. In the interests of hygiene, I'd fight off the friendly pink tongue.

It wasn't long before that baby also lay across her warm stomach at bottle time. It gave the dog a contented expression. I suppose it was a form of surrogate motherhood.

Even though she liked the baby, she really stayed the older child's pet. They would often wander off together. A boy throwing sticks for a large golden retriever with a tail that waved like a feather.

Naturally, we had our ups and downs. There was the Guy Fawkes night the dog vanished. We found her next morning several streets away, hiding in someone's garage.

There were people who accused her of relieving herself on their grass and digging holes in their herb gardens. I never believed the woman who said the dog had terrorised her child. It would have been like Mary Poppins smoking dope.

Beach holidays were the best of all. The dog swam and surfed. The ones she loved best were tortured by her rescue procedure. If you ignored her urgent barks from the shore, she'd plough out to scratch the skin off your back till you returned to the beach.

The child always worried that the dog would die one day. Pets don't last forever, so we tried to prepare him carefully. We never dreamt it would be the child who would die first.

For days after the accident, the dog lay stunned on the floor. Somehow or other, she understood what had happened. She was never quite the same again.

When we moved north to a place with next-to-no garden, the dog went to live with my mother in a smaller city. They became a familiar sight around the town. The woman who drove with a dog that sat like a queen in the back seat.

The dog was getting old and fat. But Mum didn't seem to mind the extra care and attention that was needed. They both had some loneliness to share.

She tried to fit it lightly into the telephone conversation the other day. You mustn't be upset, she said. The vet had said the emphysema attacks had got to the point where the dog couldn't go on any more.

Although we tried to hide our sorrow, we both wept softly into our receivers. The dog was another link broken with the child. We have both developed methods of coping with sadness, but sometimes they don't work.

The dog had been a joy and a nuisance; a friend and part-mother. It seemed fitting, somehow, that she had gone out wagging her tail.

Cage birds seldom inspire the passion that four-legged creatures can. Nevertheless, they're part of many households, including ours. Sometimes, the whole bird business gets out of hand.

The house is full of people wanting things. The toddler wants someone to play with her all the time. The ten year old wants someone to find his socks and listen to his times tables that never come out right.

The cat wants food all the time. If it doesn't get what it wants, it leaves a mess behind the bath where it's almost impossible to reach. The pot plants want watering. The rubbish wants putting out. So do the milk bottles. The lawn wants mowing, the cupboards want filling, the fridge wants emptying, the floor wants vacuuming. And . . .

'The budgie wants a mate.'

'What? Of course he doesn't,' I say. 'He's perfectly happy on his own.'

'No, he's not. He hardly ever sings and Alice says he'll die if he gets too lonely.'

It's not what I want to hear. But there is a mournful air about the animal as it clings to its perch and gazes through its bars.

'You should talk to it more often,' I say.

'How can I when I'm at school all day?'

Ruben, the budgie, was bought as an educational toy. The exercise wasn't cheap. The bird itself was sixteen dollars, the cage was fifty dollars and the stand was another thirty dollars. But I thought it was worth it.

The boy needed to learn to take care of things, and he was certainly doing a great job. The water was clean, the sand tray unspeckled, the cage polished to perfection. But the little blue inhabitant seemed consumed by . . . want.

'You should get him a little wife,' someone else said.

I had no idea I knew so many budgie experts.

'Last time I got a wife for a budgie he pecked her to death,' I said with a vehemence that was fashionable when feminism was at its peak.

'It can work the other way around, you know,' she said. 'Haven't you ever heard of hen pecking?'

'But the cage is too small.'

That's how we ended up back in the pet shop looking at birds again.

'We do have a sexually mature female over in the corner there,' the pet shop woman says.

When did he get so tall?

If only humans could find mates so easily.

She's bright green and fairly perky. He thinks she looks just like a Mary. When he asks the woman if our cage is suitable, she's appalled. It's barely big enough for one, let alone a courting couple.

The new cage costs sixty-five dollars on special. It won't fit the old stand. We manage to give the old cage and stand away to the girl over the back fence. She's madly in love, so she'll accept anything from our son. Even bad manners and a budgie cage.

Mary squawks indignantly in her show box all the way home. A good sign. She digs her beak into my fingers as I try to transport her tenderly into her cage.

'Blood! There's blood! You've killed her!'

With absolute horror, I see a few specks of red on her perch. Yet again, the well-meaning parent comes a cropper.

'She'll be right after she's had a little rest,' I say, cold with terror.

Next morning, it's difficult to hide my relief when we awake to find Mary still with us. In fact, she seems to have grown quite assertive. Ruben is already her slave, snuggling up to her whenever she lets him.

'All budgies want to have babies,' he says.

'But didn't you see what they look like in *The Beginner's Guide to Budgerigars?* They're all bald and slimy and they wet their nests.'

'I don't care.'

'Well, I suppose you can get a nesting box some time.'

'Budgies have seven eggs at a time, and there's not enough room for nine budgies.'

'But you give the babies away . . . or sell them to your friends . . . for five dollars each.'

He glares at me as if I've turned into a Nazi geneticist.

'When budgies have babies they want to keep them,' he says firmly. 'If you take them away they start acting weird.'

Next time he can get his educational toys from a book shop.

I guess you grow up a bit yourself as you watch your kids develop. It hit home the other night when I picked him up at the bus station after a holiday at his grandmother's.

The bus pulled in half an hour late. He was sitting where I'd expected — at the front, directly opposite the driver. We exchanged waves through the glass.

My eye automatically slid across the seat to see who had spent the past eight hours sitting next to him. Instead of the bosomy matron I had imagined, there sat a young thug of about twelve. The companion was clutching a skateboard and needed a haircut.

Funny, that. In earlier days, he always sat next to maternal-type females with knitting bags of all sorts. Maybe this time he'd had no choice.

I prepared for a major mother and child reunion. The first few days he was away, I'd enjoyed the peace. But after ten days, the house was too quiet. I almost missed seeing his shoes and underpants strewn over the living room, the blaring television, the sound of his bike clattering on the verandah.

After pushing through the crowd, I lunged forward to envelop him in my arms and bury my nose in his hair to savour that deliciously familiar perfume that is him.

Instead, he shrugged me off, took a step backward and said, 'Not here!' in hushed embarrassment.

Of course, he's right, I thought. How silly not to realise that he's reaching a Certain Age. Instead of being an extension of my body and emotions, he's beginning to see himself as his own person. He was, too, at the age of eleven. I hadn't realised how much I'd hoped it would be later rather than sooner.

'It's great to have you back!' I said, trying not to smile too broadly.

'It was really great meeting you!' he said in the same enthusiastic tone. But it wasn't for me. It was for the thug, who let out a grunt and vanished into the night.

Back home I deliberately avoided taking too much interest in his unpacking and opted for a hot soak in the bath. He came into the room to talk to me as a special privilege.

'What are you standing on?' I said, as he leant against the towel rail.

'Nothing.'

'You're having me on,' I said, propping up on my elbows. 'You're on tiptoe.'

He gave me a look that said it's not easy being the son of a lunatic. When did he get so tall?

'I've been opening doors by myself for ages, Mum. Remember?'

It happens so gradually. One day he's lying frightened and helpless in your arms. When he's small the days go on forever, like a music box tune. You can't imagine a time when we won't need nappies and 'Sweet Baby James' sung three times before he goes to sleep.

Suddenly, you wake up one day in a department store sifting through T-shirts labelled Small Men's.

He's so grown-up now, he wants adult status. But grown-ups don't consider him ready to join their conversations. He sits quietly in one corner, turning a model aircraft in one hand and sipping coffee (which he hates, but won't admit it) with the other.

He'll then let out a piercingly perceptive remark, which is likely . to send guests scuttling home for shelter.

'Go to your room!' I yell when the child inside the giant gets too irritating. But how can you say it to someone who will soon be towering over you?

'That's the last time you say go to your room to me,' he says.

And I guess he's right. It's frightening to think the blueprint has been set. Of course, I made major mistakes. I didn't talk or read to him enough, and I never worked out the discipline thing.

He's turning outside the family now for his perception of the world. What if I didn't equip him well enough? There's no starting again.

'That's the last time I do your paper round for you,' I say.

And I guess I'm wrong.

'I'll pay you,' he says hopefully.

Mothers and sons are complicated things. It's a foolish young woman who thinks she can break the bond simply by marrying him and blaming all his faults on Mum.

I'm not allowed to say I love him any more, but I am permitted to tell him when he looks good. I'm the only person allowed to study the beginnings of pimples at close range.

He expects me to act my age, 103, in public, and I'm not allowed to ask if he's changed his underwear any more. He expects me to stay in the waiting room while he visits the doctor.

To the casual observer, it might seem as if we are growing apart. But sons and mothers aren't that easy to suss out. So there.

22

Mother duck blues

IF I kept a diary, today would have a red ring around it. Not because it's anyone's birthday, or because whoever steals our newspaper in the mornings has forgotten to do it. Today is special because I put a pot plant on the floor.

It may sound like a perfectly normal act. There are thousands of people who have pot plants sitting on their carpets. In fact, for many years, I did it, too.

Then the baby started to get mobile. She dismantled the magazine rack, knocked cups off coffee tables . . . and started eating pot plants. At first, it was just the leaves. I decided she had a deficient diet and started upping her portions of silver beet and broccoli. But her interest extended to the sludgy black earth the plants sit in, and the gritty little stones.

Some parents make their lives misery by turning into disciplinarians at this stage. They think if they slap the baby's hand and yell 'No!' often enough, it will suddenly understand the value of pot plants and their delicate hold on life.

Babies don't do that. If they're hit often enough, they learn to associate the love their parents give them with pain (which is why some of them grow up to be sado-masochists). And they still keep heading for the pot plant.

It's far simpler and kinder to put all the pot plants on tables and shelves, along with all the stereo equipment, radios, magazines and coffee cups you've had to move up there as well.

Understanding people will know that houses with toddlers develop a tide mark, as valuable possessions creep higher up the wall. The bigger the baby, and the better it gets at climbing, the higher the tide mark grows. Sir Edmund Hillary's mother must have had a terrible time.

Those who are ignorant will politely suggest you go to night classes in interior decoration. There's no point in trying to explain anything to them. They're either so old they've forgotten what kids do to houses, or so young they've still got it coming.

The first few months of a baby's life are bliss as far as the furnishings go. Apart from the odd gloopy patch on the sofa, everything stays as if the place was inhabited by normal people. The first-time mother is likely to be lulled into a false sense of security, imagining she's the only person on earth who can have kids and keep a house clean.

Humans, however, aren't able to appreciate a good thing. They urge their offspring first to smile, then to reach for things, to sit alone and crawl. They're so obsessed with their baby's development, they write it all down in blue books with roses on the cover, and imagine things have happened before they have.

'My baby's been crawling since she was four months old,' said one mother admiringly, as we admired her child who appeared cast on the floor. 'I know it looks like swimming, but it's really crawling. You should have seen her this morning.'

It isn't till the small, gnome-like thing learns to pull itself up on a coffee table that a parent feels a slight pang of anxiety. The determination on its face is enough to tell parents it wasn't their coaxing so much as the child's stainless steel will that got it to this stage.

'That's lovely, dear,' you say. 'Now just lie down and say goo again.'

But once a baby has discovered the coffee table, it will never lie down and say goo again.

Shakespeare said there were seven stages of man. He must have been a lousy observer. Children go through at least one hundred stages before they're ready for school. There's the worm stage, the caterpillar stage, the eyeballs-that-work-in-different-directions stage and that's only the first few hours of life.

It isn't till we get adult and boring that there's so little to notice. Maybe that's where Shakespeare came unstuck. He should have looked at kids more closely.

It's perfectly okay to ask a woman if her baby is potty trained yet, but it's far from acceptable to ask the rattlesnake sitting next to you at a dinner if he's had his mid-life crisis yet. Adults are hung up about their own stages of growth, so they focus on their ever-changing children.

Clouds of happiness

I feel a sense of order and calm looking at the pot plant on the living room floor. As it's unlikely there will be any more babies in the house, it's probably the last time I'll have to lower the tide mark.

The baby has some sense now. She knows the pot plant isn't for eating. Just when I'm about to pour a gin in the kitchen to celebrate, there's an ominous thud from the living room. I run in there to find the pot plant prostrate on the floor. Black earth has spilled all over the carpet. A plump female child is sitting astride the remains of the pot plant's slender trunk.

'Horsy!' she says.

Her smile is too engaging for me to be mad. Besides, the theorists would say she's going through the stage where she's developing an imagination.

Only one thing is more distressing than having a small child tear your house apart. That's when it gets mysteriously unwell.

The baby is sick. She has to be, because she woke at 5 a.m. in a terrible temper. She usually sits up in her cot and smiles the day in at around 7 a.m. Today she's squirming on her stomach and going 'Whaaa! Whaa!'

Why haven't they invented babies that arrive with 2000-word vocabularies? It's a terrible design fault that makes them take so long to talk sensibly. Five in the morning isn't good. Specially seeing I didn't get to bed till 1 a.m. Vague recollections of someone licking wine off my arm at the office party fade in the stony light of dawn. If I hadn't gone out, she probably wouldn't have got sick in the first place.

I pick up her writhing body and try to make cheerful conversation. 'Whaaa!' she replies, and her eyes almost disappear behind the tear-stained cheeks.

Maybe it's a nightmare. Or teeth? It isn't allowed to be teeth any more. The men who write the baby books say too many mothers have misdiagnosed dire and perilous illnesses as teething.

It could be appendicitis. As I change her napkin, I tentatively knead her abdomen. There's no change in the 'Whaa!'

When a baby behaves like this during the day, it's so much more manageable. Only in the lonely shadows of dawn do the symptoms become sinister, and you look up the accident and emergency number in the phone book.

Mother duck blues

Babies are terrifying things. They lose heat and fluid more quickly than humans do. They're vulnerable, totally dependent. Yet they have built-in self-destruct mechanisms that make them climb concrete steps and try to swallow bees. It's impossible to manage such creatures perfectly. Yet we're supposed to.

'Whaa!' says the infant on my hip as I heat up a bottle in the kitchen.

Maybe she's hungry. This could be the start of a whole new routine of 5 a.m. starts. Or could it be a reaction to her injection? But they said to expect something three days after, not seven.

I put her back to bed, wind up her music box and crawl under my quilt. I pretend to relax in the dark silence. The walls are creaking. A cat yowls in the garden. I refuse to hear them. My entire being is centred on drifting deeper into a mystical world of . . .

'Whaaa!'

She's definitely sick. But as I peer at the centigrades, she hasn't got a temperature. At least, I think she hasn't. Thirty-six degrees doesn't mean much to me.

Last time we went to the doctor, it was humiliation. He peeked in her ears with his little light, glared at me and said she had a bad infection in both ears. He could tell I was the sort of mother who fed her baby out of cans and didn't make homemade rusks. He knew I was the layabout type who'd go to offices parties in full knowledge that the baby had ears brewing.

'Are your ears sore?' I say to the few-toothed mouth that's yelling at me.

She pauses — for breath? No, to put one finger thoughtfully in her ear. That's it! At 8.45 I ring the medical centre. The answerphone tells me to phone another number seeing it's Sunday. A bright male voice answers and says he'll be open in half an hour.

The baby starts to cheer up in the car on the way to the urgent medical centre. She even has the cheek to sing.

When we get to the waiting room, I'm almost relieved that she looks glum again and puts a stubby finger in each ear. The baby opposite is obviously quite unwell. He has a nasty cough that grates on the spine. Well, ears can be as bad as coughs.

'What's the trouble?' says the handsome young doctor.

'Goo!' she says, batting her eyelids.

Clouds of happiness

'She's been screaming and I'm sure it's ears again,' I say.

'Temperature?' says Dr Kildare, screwing his little torch together.

'No.'

'Loose?'

'Once last night,' I lie because I'm beginning to feel a fool, which is almost as bad as being a layabout.

'Off her food?'

'She didn't have any breakfast,' I say, because I was in such a panic I forgot to give her any.

'Well, there's nothing wrong with this ear,' he says. 'And this one's perfectly normal.'

She gurgles seductively as he checks out her chest and throat.

'Thank you so much,' I say, writing the cheque. 'It's so reassuring.'

The doctor smiles indulgently. Obviously a neurotic, he thinks. Thank God she's not on my books.

Going back home in the car, she sings her version of 'Baa Baa Black Sheep'. I feel like going 'Whaaa!'

She likes the park. It's as if this chubby little thing understands she's part of the new life that bursts out around her here. Armed with a plastic bag full of bread, we've come to see the ducks. My own duckling with her fluffy yellow hair sticking out behind, waddles across the cellophane green grass.

'Have more fear!' I want to say as she marches up to a malevolent black swan.

'Duck,' she says, pointing at its sharp red beak.

It spreads its wings, fixes me with a threatening eye and hisses. The swan and I recognise an unreasoning passion in each other. It's called motherhood. No words are exchanged, but we both know if either touches the other's young, the fight will be to the death.

I pull my duckling aside, and she bellows with rage. Distant swans let out their pathetic cries. It seems they're either indulging in outrageous self-pity, or being downright nasty.

A squadron of ducks flies overhead. Willows languish in the dappled water. The bushes are rustling with activity, as if someone is creating something under every leaf. A pair of human lovers is entwined on the grass.

Mother duck blues

A battalion of geese spies our plastic bag and prepares for assault.

'Duck!' the baby says, running gleefully to the geese.

I was brought up to believe geese are unworthy creatures, also prone to hissing and bad temper. If they don't get their way, they can flap their wings and break your arm. Or is that swans? Either way, the geese have unintelligent blue eyes and they're pushy. Best off in pâté.

'Let's find the ducks,' I say to the toddler, who seems nonplussed.

As we turn to walk away, the geese put their beaks in the air and head off in the opposite direction, as if begging for food was the last thing on their minds. At least they have dignity. I begin to feel ashamed. The line between greed and need is so fine. Surely a pushy goose is as deserving of mouldy bread as an elusive duck?

'Duck!' the baby says to the nervous sparrows that bob around our feet. The ducks are hard to find. Black swans and their huddles of whistling white babies have taken over the lake. I think back to my childhood when black swans were rare, exotic creatures to be much admired and sought out among the white.

Now the white swans have disappeared. Black is beautiful, but a combination is best. They seem to specialise in two-parent families — mother and father aggressively ensuring their cygnets' survival. Maybe that's their secret.

Further around the lake, we meet pheasants. Always in pairs, my father used to say. As a result, I've admired the birds for their ability to find the secret to happy marriage when so much of the world seems to have failed. I offer them bread and mutter respectfully.

'Duck!' the toddler says, pointing at their ancient-looking feet.

Suddenly, there's a bloodcurdling squawk as one large male attacks his mate, pummels the bread out of her beak and shoos her away. He smooths his ruffled feathers and tries to put on a look he imagines is appealing. I glare down at him. I had no idea his breed were such wife bashers. Must all illusions shatter?

A gaggle of adolescent schoolgirls strolls past.

'And then I said . . . and then *he* said . . . !' and they dissolve in giggles.

My own duckling terrifies me with her hunger for adventure.

She wants to see, hear and smell all of the world at once. And she wants to swim in it.

'Come back!' I call to the sturdy little figure. To her, come back means something exciting is only seconds away and someone is trying to stop it happening. She accelerates on the slope to the glistening lake.

I scoop her up half a footstep from the water's edge and meet the understanding eye of a mother duck. She's brown, dowdy and wrung out with the responsibility of nine ducklings who are hellbent on going in different directions.

A solo mother, too. The father is probably off across the lake having a good time with the seagulls.

'I know the type,' I say, hurling her some bread.

Even now, she puts her ducklings first, letting them eat their fill before she hungrily takes her share. The poor thing obviously never heard of rights for women. I hope this noble duck mother gets her reward somewhere. Maybe she'll be content to get a damn good rest when she gets to the big pond in the sky.

'Duck!' I say to the toddler. 'Duck! Duck!'

She crumbles some bread over her shoes from Brazil and remains silent.

23

Woman alone

AS I lay in bed last night, the sounds of an agitated argument between a man and a woman set up across the road.

We live in the sort of neighbourhood where people keep to themselves, so I didn't take much notice until the voices rose to a squawking peak. It's surprising how like barnyard chickens people sound from a distance when they're fighting. I gauged from the clarity and volume that they were now on their front steps.

'I don't want the house!' he yelled. 'You keep the house!'

A few seconds later, a car door slammed and a Volkswagen engine roared off into the night. A relieved silence settled over the street. After a few heart-pounding moments peering after his tail lights, she probably went back inside to call her best friend.

In those minutes, I got to know more about the people across the road than I have in six months of living here. I wasn't sorry not to know the events leading up to his departure, but there was something poignant about the fact that I don't even know their names.

If the same thing had happened fifty or even one hundred years ago, when this row of workers' cottages was built, everyone in the neighbourhood would have known, cared and gossiped terribly about the incident. The night Tom, Harry or Brian left would have kept the almost identical kitchens buzzing for months.

Where people once treasured a friendly neighbourhood, nowadays they seem to value anonymity. The houses are only a metre or two apart. If I'm in the garden, I can hear the loo flushing next door. From their bathroom window, they have a too-clear view of our hot tub.

But we play it cool. Polite nods at the front gate and no more. While there is a Neighbourhood Watch sticker on their front door, there's the understanding we won't watch too closely, or get too involved.

One of the reasons the street is colourful is it's only partly yuppified. There are still immigrants and people who rent. It won't be long before ambitious young professionals buy those homes to strip the floorboards, expose the fireplaces and fit German kitchens.

In the old days, the elderly woman on the other side would have been almost revered as a character. The paint on her house is peeling off faster than a summer tan. The name Gigi is hammered above her front door — a legacy from the 50s when people were frivolous enough to name their houses after sex symbols.

I discovered the reason why she never goes outside when I was locked out one day. I took the toddler and tapped on her door to ask to use the phone. I was astonished to find her door ajar. You're supposed to lock everything in the street.

The air was stale and musky in the darkened hallway. A quavery voice called from the bedroom. I was unprepared for such a sad sight. She was curled up on her bed, her limbs thin and brittle like candy. Her nightdress, which was tousled like a wild sea, revealed drooping black stockings held up by suspenders.

One of her painful red eyes swivelled up to the ceiling while the other gazed at me through an oily film. When she beckoned us closer, the toddler screamed and ran outside.

'It's since her husband died,' said a voice behind. 'She hasn't been outside for ten years.'

A visiting niece in her 20s guided me to the phone. I now understood the too-hearty cries of the meals-on-wheels matron. The hooting sounds she makes from the front gate mean she's working up courage to go in. Some days, I've seen the matron scuttling down the path, ducking to avoid projectiles that are being hurled after her.

I met another neighbour at 2 a.m. when we were both in dressing gowns. I'd been unable to encourage the man of the house to tell the geriatric hippies across the road to turn down their rock concert. So I stormed onto the verandah, Boadicea-like, to do battle.

It was a great relief to see another woman already hammering at their door begging them to stop. As we stood ghostlike in the moonlight, another historic change seemed apparent.

In the old days, our husbands would have been out there instead. We two working women with kids value sleep above all else. We have been trained not to expect our men to protect us any more.

'It could have started a fight if I'd gone out,' he said, snuggling his feminist folds into the waterbed.

'Well, I could have been raped.'

On the whole, I enjoy the unpredictable vitality of this street. It's not the sort of neighbourhood where people drop in to borrow a cup of sugar. There aren't many of those left, anyway.

As the gap between the sexes becomes more apparent, it's important that women don't regard men as enemies. Sometimes, however, it's not easy.

The sky was turning gold in the west. I'd been promising myself a walk since lunchtime, but there had been an avalanche of interruptions. If I didn't get that stroll along the beach now, darkness would set in. I'd go to sleep regretting that I hadn't set eyes on the cool, glistening water and let the breeze iron out the lines on my forehead.

As I strode across the street, I felt guilty for being so free. It was the first thing I'd done for at least a week that didn't involve someone else — the baby, the eleven year old, the office, a friend.

For once, I belonged entirely to me. Although I wouldn't always want to be that way, the sensation was exhilarating.

The beach was a private place. I discovered it by accident with the kids one day. We trailed down the path, half-thinking it would end in someone's back garden. But it led us on through leafy twists and bends, down several flights of steps to the water. The tide was high that day and the water was laughing and slapping the steps.

This time I wanted to go there on my own to take deep breaths and get ready for another week. I hurried down the path, looking forward to the moment I'd be alone with the sea. Around the last corner to the top of the steps and . . . my heart stopped. The tide was out.

It hadn't occurred to me that someone else would be there. He took huge steps across the rockpools, like a confident giant. His hair was untidy and he wore a red and black bush jacket. His muscular bare legs ended in a pair of sandshoes. More than anything, his brightly coloured socks caught my eye. Perhaps he played rugby.

My annoyance at finding him there quickly gave way to

something else. The recent upsurge in rapes and assaults on women has been heavily reported in newspapers and on the air waves. Police say that on top of that, an astounding number go unrecorded.

The days when rape was regarded as a bizarre, virtually unheard-of crime are over. It's getting to the point where some say a woman walking alone at night is asking for trouble.

The young man in socks was probably harmless. But he was strong. What if he'd come down to the beach to lurk, maybe even with a knife in his pocket?

I tried to remember the things I'd learnt at self-defence classes. Never look like a potential victim. I fluffed out my coat and marched out to the shoreline. Be tall, intimidating. Never look anxiously over your shoulder.

I glanced anxiously over my shoulder. He was pretending I wasn't there because:

a) he knew how frightened I was and was trying not to make things worse, or

b) he always did that before the attack.

I wondered how a magistrate would regard the situation. Had I provoked assault merely by walking alone in the evening? If women invite disaster by doing such things, then every man must be regarded as a potentially violent, sex-crazed lunatic.

The era of chastity belts and princesses in towers seems civilised by comparison.

Although it's the minority who attack and are attacked, the increase in rape creates a rift between women and men. Perhaps it's wise to be suspicious in some cases, but I still recall the bewildered look on a friend's face when he was told firmly but kindly the babysitting club preferred women to care for the kids. I wonder what percentage of suburban dads really are likely to interfere with the neighbourhood kids?

Is the man in the children's swimming pool a concerned parent or a child molester?

Men could do with a dollop of good publicity at the moment. If they're as concerned about their image as they should be, it's time they did something to remind the world they are husbands, lovers and fathers who are also appalled and outraged by those who rape.

One of the most heartwarming photos I've ever seen was one of men trailing kids and pushing prams as they marched against rape. Maybe it's time they marched again.

There are other, less dramatic ways men can help restore their women's faith. They need to speak out more readily against sexism in advertising and sexual violence on television and in film.

I tried to hold my ground on the beach, to act as if I had a right to be there. But my heart was pounding in my ears.

Earlier that day, a male friend had been for a walk in the bush. He'd come back saying it was great. He'd seen only one other person — a man. It seemed crazy that his pleasure of sharing the landscape with another human should be my terror, simply because we have different genders.

I almost ran back up the steps. The sock-horror man didn't follow. He kept striding over the rockpools as if he owned them.

And I suppose he did.

Our great-grandmothers would probably have problems identifying with today's young women. A husband and family is no longer all we dream of. We want careers, equality, companionship and emotional intimacy. It may seem too much to expect. Those who try to be the perfect wife, mother, employee and friend are under enormous pressure. It's hardly surprising that often at least one area snaps under the strain.

As a result, women alone are becoming a familiar sight. Many turn to women friends for the closeness they had hoped to find with men. Some are beginning to wonder if men and women are best off living together at all. Perhaps the answer is to call a truce, live apart and visit each other often.

A woman on her own is still a bit of a freak. People act as if she's too self-sufficient, or maybe even too loose to make friends with.

The resort hotel bar was full of ruddy-faced men shouting at their mates. The wives cowered in corners and didn't invite smiles of conspiracy. They seemed engrossed in their own problems — raising ungrateful children and putting up with their husbands' oafishness.

Yes, it's a man's world up here. They look amiable enough with their curly sideburns and comical fishing hats. But they talk to women in the sharp, clipped tones most people reserve for dogs.

Photographs of dead marlins hung up by their tails took pride of place on the walls. There's a shot of the day some hero drove a jeep into the bar. A well-meaning poem about the arrival of a local male child.

A woman alone wants to make excuses. To explain she's not here to sell her body to the locals, break up families and spread disease. That she's not eccentric, unlovable or untrustworthy. She's just here for a change of scenery.

Only the barman seemed to understand my isolation. He gave me an orange juice with ice for free. Our conversation ran dry soon after. The woman who ran the dining room peered over her half-moon spectacles to the non-existent partner behind my shoulder. The large room was empty. Red fans of table napkins roosted like birds on white tablecloths.

'Have you booked?' No.

She said she could fit me in and directed me to a discreet table for two wedged between the bar and the kitchen. As I studied the menu over a glass of wine for one, regulation people drifted into the room. The group of haw-hawing yachtsmen, a fiftyish couple with identical turned-down mouths.

I recognised the pair of effeminate gentlemen from earlier that day. They'd been on the motel beach. But when I said, 'We meet again!', they blushed and recoiled. Invisibility was something they craved this weekend.

An extremely self-satisfied young couple were given the table next to mine. They didn't seem married. She fiddled with the orchid centrepiece, fixed him with a drilling eye and said, 'Didn't I give you one of these once?'

Yes, he said without conviction after a silence. He seemed vague, mildly confused. She tougher, more resilient. I assumed his money-making potential was vast. She ogled him like a crocodile and flashed me a Keep Off smile.

Soon after, the comfortably sized waitress put two young men at another nearby table. By young, I mean they were about eleven or twelve. One had braces on his teeth, which had no effect on his self-confidence.

'I'll have the calamari,' he said imperiously. 'And the steak. And make sure I get plenty of chips.'

The two young men eyed each other gleefully. They were obviously in training for a seat in the bar next door.

'Have you written it down?'

'I will when I get into the kitchen,' she said.

A woman alone could hardly be incriminated for talking to twelve year olds.

'Are you two gentlemen staying here?' I asked.

They shot me a satirical look and said yes.

'No, actually,' the quieter one said. 'Our dad has shares in this place.'

The waitress reappeared and placed the calamari dishes in front of them.

'I'll kill you if I don't get a heap of chips,' said the boy with braces.

I couldn't help wondering if he could do with heaps of something else. With amazing good humour, she drifted to another part of the room. The little Lords Fauntleroy picked up the calamari rings in their hands and dipped them in a bottle of sauce. The one with braces looked at me sideways and said, 'What are you, a professional observer, or something?'

I put my head down and tried to mind my own business. Just then, the waitress swooped on them like a shark let loose in a goldfish tank.

'If I catch you eating those with your fingers, you're dead meat!' she said.

They dropped their food and smirked, guiltily. But she didn't hang around to see. She swept out. The kitchen door slammed with a gush of wind.

At least one woman around here was prepared to stand up for herself.

24

The happiness cloud

EVERY AGE has its fashion that falls flat. In the 50s, they had the hula hoop. It seemed like a lot of fun at the time. People could have been excused for thinking their descendants would be wiggling their hips inside rings of cane for centuries to come.

But the hula hoop didn't have the ingredients of a classic. Maybe it took too much energy, or perhaps it was basically a stupid idea.

In the 60s, it looked as if false eyelashes would last forever. Those who didn't sport extra eye hair looked as if they'd been in a recent laboratory explosion.

The tricky little things had their draw-backs, too. They were likely to peel off at inconvenient times, and nobody was comfortable sleeping with the things on. It wasn't by accident that eyelashes became less popular, the more determinedly promiscuous people became. Only the sight of plastic teeth by the bedside could be less appealing than a pair of huge, gummy winkers curled up like discarded caterpillars.

The flop of the 70s had to be open marriage. It used to be a wonderfully successful way to open conversation at social gatherings. An appalling old alligator would sidle up to you and say . . .

'My wife and I have an open marriage.'

Closer scrutiny usually revealed that only one partner was aware he or she was part of an open marriage. The other one usually stayed at home watching television and waiting for their mate's spate of working late to finish.

There used to be a lot of people, usually women, with long-suffering smiles at those gatherings. It wasn't easy belonging to an open marriage.

To make matters worse, the best openly married couples knew it was All Right As Long As You Talked About It. It made them feel better, and much less guilty, to deliver blow-by-blow accounts of their latest fling to anyone who would listen, including their spouse. The inevitable pain and tears were supposed to be a Growing Experience.

They conveniently overlooked the fact that no matter how logical and understanding people would be in an ideal world, human frames weren't made to be subjected to such tirades of repressed jealousy and anxiety.

In most cases, open marriages followed a natural progression to being closed divorces.

The fashion didn't go out with a bang. It just fizzled away rather like the hula hoop. Very few people still keep hula hoops in the garage and only a few couples can say they tried open marriage and survived.

The two words don't really belong together, anyway. The main reason people get married in the first place is to ensure their partners focus most of their attention on that relationship. It's difficult enough to maintain warmth and friendship through the years without throwing a time bomb into the contract.

We can thank AIDS and the new morality for the fact that men no longer sneak up to women to talk about open marriage. It's a relief to be entering an era when even James Bond is a one-woman man.

Like everyone else on the planet, Bond and his chosen one will have to learn the delights of romance and conversational foreplay. It will be interesting to watch Bond extend his vocabulary. A challenge for him to stop reaching for his zip the moment he sets eyes on a woman.

Those who are tempted to stray are now burdened not only with the passion-stifling gymnastics that accompany condoms, but with the spectre of deceit. It's a concept our ancestors were well aware of. It means lies, guilt and enough stress to give anyone cancer.

Perhaps it would help if people had a more realistic picture of marriage. It was comparatively simple for Elizabethans to say 'till death us do part' when they were likely to die before the age of thirty.

Life has a habit of changing people as they grow older. In a few extraordinary cases, people grow together. In most cases, however, wife and husband experience life in different ways. He's under pressure to be rich, powerful, a real man. She must cope with the majority of the demands of childbearing, mothering, housekeeping — and now, running a career of her own.

Clouds of happiness

Only the elderly say there should be a law against young marriage. They've forgotten the intensity of the romance, not to mention the sex drive, of the younger years.

Young couples need to know that eternity is rather a huge idea — that making a go of a monogamous relationship for as long as possible can still be considered a success.

At least their thoughts won't be clouded with the idea of open marriage. The whole thing created more discomfort than false eyelashes, more embarrassment than the hula hoop and a damn sight more frustration and confusion than the Rubik's Cube. Thank heavens the book on open marriage can now be discreetly shut.

I once read that everyone marries again in their 30s. They either marry the same person, or they marry someone else. A lot of women I know seem trapped between the two.

A good man is hard to find. At least, that's what a lot of women are saying. Everywhere, there are attractive, scintillating, well-paid women who simply can't find a mate. Some of them are beginning to wonder if all the eligible men have taken off to live in a far-off land that women haven't yet discovered.

In the meantime, a lot of high-powered dynamic females are left languishing over their briefcases, wondering if a decent relationship will ever turn up.

'Men are scared of me,' says one career-oriented solo mother. 'But I'm darned if I'm going to pretend I'm less capable than I really am. I've worked very hard to have a career and kids.'

Women like her, in their 30s and 40s and longing for some sparkle in their lives, meet each other for lunch and the sort of laughter and companionship they'd like to get from men.

'Married or gay?' they ask automatically when an interesting man turns up in conversation.

Sometimes, they wonder if they're demanding too much, but they don't want a child–man who'll suck away the strength they have mustered, often quite painfully. Many women have shaken their lives by the scruff of the neck to give themselves a chance for independence and happiness.

It doesn't seem unreasonable to refuse to be dominated and told what to do, when to cook and where to live. It can't be too much to expect a man to listen and understand, sometimes.

The happiness cloud

Women who are working at getting their lives together want someone to enjoy their considerable accomplishments without being threatened, share their company and kids and exchange some intimacy and loving.

'I always assumed I'd find a man as soon as I got divorced,' says another. 'But most male executives of my level don't want someone like me. I'd be too demanding. I understand them in a way. They want someone they can nip home to when they feel like it. Someone who won't complain.'

However, even the meekest of females are beginning to rebel. Women of all descriptions are fed up with men who don't listen, won't talk and refuse to get emotionally close.

Many people are surprised when surveys show that large numbers of women are unhappy in their marriages. But to most women, it's no surprise. So often, the male is better at taking than giving, at being comforted than giving comfort.

Once upon a time, his pay cheque was supposed to make up for the hollow loneliness many wives felt. Now women have learnt to make their own money, they have more power. Power to reject limpingly inadequate marriages. Large numbers of women are initiating their own divorces.

The old stereotype of women desperately clinging to their mates has almost vanished. In many cases now, it's the men who try to hang on to a faltering relationship.

Talking and listening seems such a basic contribution to a relationship, yet the male's refusal to listen is the biggest cause of women's anger. When she tries to get through to him, he accuses her of nagging, whistles, reads the paper or goes 'out'.

It can hardly come as a shock then that huge numbers of women in long-term marriages have given up trying to draw out the sullen, monosyllabic men in their lives. Many women are calling it quits and concentrating on the things that can give satisfaction — kids, friends and jobs.

In many cases, that means learning to live alone. It's not an easy prospect when we're brought up with the dream of being able to share our deepest feelings with a male — who'll be as good in bed as he is at mending fuses.

'Living alone is great once you get used to it,' said a divorced friend. 'You cook your meals when you like, go for walks when you want. Nobody bosses you around or complains about your friends coming over.'

Although she painted a picture of serenity and strength, I probed further to find she hoped it wouldn't always be that way. That one day a caring, funny, intelligent man would decide to pitch his tent at her place.

Women alone in relationships and alone by themselves make the most of their women friends. There's much to be said for loyal companionship, laughs and people who understand.

Men have come a long way in recent years. Many have learnt to be caring fathers and housepersons. But they'll have to move faster still if they're to keep up with their women. Or perhaps men will feel they've done all they can and the sexes will retreat into separate camps.

'After all, males don't do much in the jungle, do they?' says another woman friend. 'They just hang around for a bit of insemination and that's it.'

In the meantime, women who are unhappy with their marriages are wondering if they should bother putting so much energy into love relationships — and are voting with their feet.

I saw a crystal ball in a shop window this afternoon. It wasn't so much a ball as a pendant. The sort you hang in your window to spread rainbows throughout your room, life or whatever.

They're supposed to give spiritual strength. There are times when I could do with a dose of it. Shame they don't sell it in bottles.

Gypsies used to see the future in crystal balls. Sometimes, I wonder what would happen if every human foetus could check out his or her future life with a thing like that. How many would choose to take on the assault course ahead?

But I guess it's worth the effort if you have something to offer the planet — whether it's understanding other people, or something intensely practical, like knowing how to help plants grow.

Earth needs people with a sense of hope because there's a lot of mess to clean up. The human race has committed disgraceful crimes against the landscape and its life forms. Huge amounts of energy must go into undoing the technological and industrial disasters we've created.

While nuclear arms still exist, we're doing away with the possibility of any future. The issue must be dealt with now, because there will be no time to sort the mess out after it's happened. Time will not exist.

The big things have to be faced and sorted out in a world that could change beyond recognition at the push of a button.

At a personal level, however, everyone is still seeking the elusive thing humanity has always craved. Happiness exists because you know how it feels when you have it. But it's rather like a fluffy white cloud in the sky. You know it's there because you can see it. But if you try to catch it in your hand and lock it in a box, it simply evaporates.

It's pointless to try to possess something so fast-moving and changeable. Better, perhaps, to be the thing instead of trying to own it.

A cloud races across the sky and changes shape and colour. It reflects the lavish reds of sunset, turns to steel and weeps silvery tears in storms. Yet it remains free.

None of us is much more permanent than the clouds. Marriages dissolve and people you love die. But there isn't much time for analysis and self-pity. Everyone has things to do while they're here.

It's a matter of adjusting and changing shape to cope with the storms, and remembering how to glow golden in a sunrise. You have to let go of the ones who have left and look forward to the ones who haven't turned up yet.

Somehow, you have to negate bitterness and believe love is still possible.